Cambridge English

Compact

GW00648320

Preliminary for Schools

Student's Book

Sue Elliott and Amanda Thomas

CAMBRIDGE
UNIVERSITY PRESS

University Printing House, Cambridge CB2 8BS, United Kingdom

Cambridge University Press is part of the University of Cambridge.

It furthers the University's mission by disseminating knowledge in the pursuit of education, learning and research at the highest international levels of excellence.

www.cambridge.org
Information on this title: www.cambridge.org/9781107694095

© Cambridge University Press 2013

First published 2013
8th printing 2014

Printed in the United Kingdom by Latimer Trend

A catalogue record for this publication is available from the British Library

ISBN 978-1-107-69409-5 Student's Book without answers with CD-ROM
ISBN 978-1-107-61027-9 Teacher's Book
ISBN 978-1-107-63539-5 Workbook without answers with Audio CD
ISBN 978-1-107-66714-3 Student's Pack
ISBN 978-1-107-63262-2 Class Audio CD
ISBN 978-1-107-69233-6 Classware DVD-ROM

CONTENTS

MAP OF THE UNITS

UNIT	TOPICS	GRAMMAR	VOCABULARY
1 All about me!	Giving personal information Being at school	Present simple & present continuous *-ing* forms	School subjects Sports facilities School rooms School collocations
2 Winning & losing	Sport Hobbies & leisure	Past simple Past continuous	Phrasal verbs
3 Let's shop!	Clothes Shopping	Order of adjectives Comparing	
4 Relax!	Personal feelings Entertainment & media	Present perfect	
5 Extreme diets	Food & drink Health	Future forms	Food & drink Phrasal verbs with *go*
6 My home	House & home Places & buildings	*used* to Verbs followed by infinitive / *-ing* form *do, make, go, have*	Weather People Home Places
7 Wild at heart	The natural world Environment	Past perfect	Animals Natural world Weather
8 We're off!	Transport Travel & holidays	First & second conditional	

READING	WRITING	LISTENING	SPEAKING
Part 2: Finding an e-pal Part 5: School in 15th-century England	Part 2: Notes & emails Linking words Beginnings & endings Punctuation	Part 4: Talking about a new building for school	Part 1: Questions – asking and answering about school
Part 3: The history of BMX biking Part 5: The importance of team games	Part 3: Planning a story Correcting mistakes	Part 3: A talk about a special sports school	Part 2: A visit to a sports activity centre Agreeing and disagreeing
Part 5: An article about Harrods Part 1: Shopping	Part 3: Using pronouns *who, which, where* Pronouns for reference	Part 2: An interview with two young clothes designers	Part 4: Talking about places to shop
Part 4: My favourite movies Part 5: Learning to rock	Part 1: *just / yet / already* Word-building	Part 1: Short extracts about entertainment	Part 3: Describing people
Part 1: Food & health Part 5: Should we eat less meat?	Part 2: Modal verbs: suggesting, offering, requesting	Part 3: A talk about an extreme camping trip	Part 1: Questions – asking and answering about family and friends
Part 4: My home is a windmill Part 5: The pyramids in Egypt	Part 3: Linking words	Part 1: Seven short extracts	Part 2: Giving opinions, making suggestions, asking for opinions Things to take on a school trip to a castle
Part 5: The world's most dangerous animal Part 2: Charities working to help the environment	Part 1: Reported speech	Part 2: An interview with a zookeeper	Part 3: Describing animals and places
Part 3: My submarine trip Part 5: Holidays in space	Part 2: Describing a photo	Part 4: A conversation about a horse-riding holiday	Part 4: Talking about a holiday

All about me!

READING Giving personal information

1 Mark's class teacher wants all her students to find e-pals on the internet – students they can write to in schools in other countries. Read what Mark says about himself.

> Hi everyone! My name's Mark and I've just had my 14th birthday. I'm living in France at the moment, but I'm originally from Canada – we moved here two years ago when I started at high school. I'm not great at maths, but I still enjoy it – although what I like best is art. I love drawing at home, and using my computer in my room for playing games or contacting friends. I enjoy writing songs on my guitar, too. I'd like to perform with my friends one day! I'm not keen on doing sport, though – lots of my friends play football, but not me. I'm quite a tidy person – I haven't got many books, but I always put them away on the shelves. And people say I'm very friendly, too! I always chat to people when I take our dog for a walk.

2 Complete the information about Mark.

Name: Mark ....   Age? ....

From? ....   School? ....

Favourite lesson? ....

What does he like doing in his free time? ....

What sort of person is he? ....

3 Look at the pictures below. Which is Mark's room, do you think – A or B? Give reasons for your answer.

I think … is Mark's room, because … I don't think it's … because …

4 Read information about three possible e-pals for Mark. <u>Underline</u> details which match Mark's description in Exercise 1.

1 Tom likes sending emails and playing computer games, and wants to talk about sport with his e-pal. He'd also like to find someone who loves reading lots of different books.

2 Cris is looking for someone who's lived in a different country. He'd also like his e-pal to have similar interests to his of writing music and being a member of a band.

3 Sam wants to write to someone who's just changed schools, as he has. He also wants to find someone who is friendly and likes animals.

The teacher of the Canadian class below wants her students to find e-pals to write to in a school in Australia.

Below there are descriptions of eight Australian e-pals.

Decide which e-pal would be the most suitable for the following class members.

For questions **1–5**, mark the correct letter (**A–H**) on your answer sheet.

1  Shona likes writing stories and drawing pictures to go with them, and wants to exchange her work with her e-pal. She'd also like to find someone who enjoys sport, as she does.

2  Ryan has recently moved to Canada and is looking for someone who's also lived in a different country. He'd also like his e-pal to share his interest of making model vehicles, and spending time outdoors.

3 Connie wants to write to someone who's just changed schools, as she has. She also enjoys learning about science at school, and has lots of pets at home.

4 Robert loves watersports and wants to write to someone with the same interest. He also writes and performs his own songs at his school, and would like to send some of his songs to his e-pal.

5  Sandra wants an e-pal who's also keen on acting, as she has already been on some TV shows. She'd also like to learn how to make food from Australia.

A Hello! I'm **Sacha** and I live right near the sea, so windsurfing's very popular here, but I prefer more creative activities. I really enjoy art at school, and I can send you some pictures I've done. I keep animals at home, too – I've got six rabbits!

B Hi, I'm **Jude**, and I've just arrived in Australia, so I spend a lot of time watching TV, especially music and drama programmes. I've got a good singing voice, and I've even recorded songs myself! Listen to them on our school website!

C Hi! I'm **Alex**, and I haven't been in Australia long – I was brought up in the US. We're living in the city centre now but I miss the open spaces around our farm where we lived before. I still find time for my hobby, though – building small remote-control cars and driving them through the park.

D My name's **Bailey**, and I'm really interested in cooking – I've got lots of recipes I can share with you. I also enjoy being on stage. I've been in lots of plays and even one or two on television, so write to me if those are your interests too.

E I'm called **Charlie**, and I love singing in front of an audience! I'm always in all the musicals at my school – see our website! I'd love to hear some of your music too! My other interests are swimming and sailing – my home's near a beach so I spend every weekend there.

F I'm **Jo** and I really enjoy school. I'm good at volleyball and tennis, and I'm in the school team. I enjoy reading too, especially anything written by people my age. At the moment I'm spending lots of time doing cartoons, too. I'll send you some!

G I'm **Matty** and I've always lived in the same house, so my room's full of things I've drawn or built! I enjoy making models of radio-controlled cars and then driving them in the garden. It's helped my science studies a lot – that's my favourite subject now!

H Hi, I'm **Ray** and I love where I'm studying now. I came here from my primary school last year. There's lots more chance to study biology, which I like. I belong to a cookery club and I love animals too – I've got a dog and a cat at home!

LISTENING Being at school

Part 4

1 Put the words about places in a school under the best heading.

> ~~history~~ office tennis courts swimming pool
> maths canteen biology hall reception
> languages geography science lab
> football pitch library IT

Subjects	Sports facilities	Rooms
history		

2 Work in pairs. Use the words in Exercise 1 to describe your school.

3 🔘 02 Listen to Sarah talking about her first school. Decide if she liked (☺) or disliked (☹) each place. Tick (✔) the correct boxes.

	☺	☹
canteen		✔
gym		
playground		
swimming pool		
art room		
science lab		
garden		
Sarah's classroom		

4 Listen to Sarah again. Are these sentences correct or incorrect?

1 Sarah enjoyed lessons in the science lab.
2 Sarah's classroom was painted a dark colour.
3 If Sarah worked hard, she could go for a swim in the summer.

5 Match the verbs in the box with the phrases about being at school.

> eat work hand in wear ~~attend~~ get
> go to pass play perform go on arrive

~~attend~~ classes each day
.... hard
.... good grades
.... a uniform every day
.... football for the team
.... an after-school club
.... on stage
.... homework on time
.... school trips
.... exams
.... a packed lunch
.... late for school

6 🔘 03 Listen to Sarah talking about the rules at her school. Are these sentences correct or incorrect?

1 Sarah wears a uniform.
2 Sarah arrives at school on time.
3 Sarah plays football.

7 Work in pairs. How do you have to behave at your school? Tell your partner if you like or dislike the rules. Use some of the phrases in Exercise 5 and *have to, don't have to.*

> We have to be at school by 8.20 a.m.
> I don't have to get up that early!

Exam task

Exam tip

Read through the sentences first, then listen carefully for the opinions of the speakers. ✓

🔘 04 Look at the six sentences for this part. You will hear a conversation between a boy, Jake, and a girl, Holly, about a new hall at their school. Decide if each sentence is correct or incorrect. If it is correct, put a tick (✔) in the box under **A** for **YES**. If it is not correct, put a tick (✔) in the box under **B** for **NO**.

		YES	NO
1	Jake found it difficult to imagine the new hall before he saw it.	A ☐	B ☐
2	Jake and Holly agree that their old school hall needed replacing.	A ☐	B ☐
3	Holly was sorry to see part of their sports field used for building.	A ☐	B ☐
4	Holly is positive about the environmentally-friendly heating in the hall.	A ☐	B ☐
5	Jake is looking forward to a classical music concert in the hall.	A ☐	B ☐
6	They both want to get involved in a future event in the hall.	A ☐	B ☐

1 SPEAKING

Part 1

1 **Match the two halves of questions about school, then ask and answer with your partner.**

1	Where	a	enjoy learning English?
2	How	b	did you start at your school?
3	What	c	is your school?
4	Do you	d	got a swimming pool at your school?
5	Have you	e	do you get to school every day?
6	Are you	f	speak more than two languages?
7	When	g	happy at school?
8	Can you	h	is your favourite subject?

2 **How do you say these letters?**

A C G I B E J W Y P

3 **Work in pairs. Take turns to spell out these names.**

1 S–M–I–T–H **2** J–O–H–N–S–O–N **3** W–Y–A–T–T **4** G–O–R–D–O–N

🔘 **05** Now listen and check your answers.

4 🔘 **06** Listen and write down the names you hear.

5 **Work in pairs. Spell out the following. Write down what your partner says.**

a your surname
b your best friend's surname
c the name of your street
d the name of your favourite shop

6 **Match the examiner's questions with a short answer from A. Then find a longer answer from B that develops what you want to say.**

Question
1 Do you like English?
2 Where do you live?
3 Tell us about your English teacher.
4 What do you enjoy doing in the evening?
5 Tell us about your family.

A
There are three of us.
Watching TV.
Yes.
Italy.
Her name's Tina.

B
She's young and friendly and she makes us laugh!
My mum's a nurse and my dad works in an office.
In a small town called Chiavari.
The grammar is difficult, though.
My favourite programmes are music shows.

7 **Look at the beginnings of some answers for Speaking Part 1 questions. How could you develop them?**

1 I'm from ....
2 At the moment, I'm studying ....
3 I live ....
4 In my spare time I ....
5 In my family there are ....
6 Last Saturday I ....

Exam task

🔘 **07** Listen to the examiner's questions and answer when your teacher pauses the recording.

> **Exam tip**
>
> To get good marks in the Speaking Test, you need to develop your answers as much as you can. ✓

GRAMMAR

Present simple & present continuous

G *Page 78*

1 Look at what Mark and Sarah say, then complete rules 1–3 with these phrases.

> things that are happening now   the present continuous
> routines – things we do every day

Mark: I haven't got many books, but I always **put** them away on the shelves.

Sarah: We **go** to school from 8 a.m. to 2.30 p.m. every day.

Mark: I'**m writing** an essay about France at the moment.

Mark: I **come** from Canada but I'**m living** in France now because my father's working here.

1 We use the **present simple** to talk about ....
2 We use the **present continuous** to talk about ....
3 To talk about something that is **temporary** we use ....

2 Read Amy's diary for today. Cross out the <u>incorrect</u> verb forms.

At the moment (0) ~~I write~~ / I'm writing this diary.
(1) I sit / I'm sitting on my bed and (2) watch / watching
TV too. It's my favourite programme - Pop Stuff!
(3) I watch / I'm watching it every Friday evening at 6.00,
after (4) I get / I'm getting home from swimming club.
I've got a drink, so (5) I try / I'm trying to drink that and
(6) I write / I'm writing at the same time - it's not easy!
(7) Mum cooks / Mum's cooking the dinner - she's just
said it'll be ready soon. It'll probably be a big family dinner with roast
chicken - (8) she usually makes / she's usually making that every Friday as
(9) she never has / she's never having time during the week. Anyway,
(10) we work and study / we're working and studying so hard at the moment
that we're hardly ever all at home at the same time!

3 Now talk with your partner. What's happening now in her house, according to Amy? What happens regularly?

What about you? Think of some things that a) you do regularly b) you're doing now.

4 ⊙ Exam candidates often make mistakes with the present simple and present continuous. Correct the mistakes in these sentences.

1 ~~I write~~ to you to answer your letter. I'm *writing*
2 We are planing to see a new film this evening.
3 I am wanting to see that film too.
4 I'm having exams every day at school.
5 My favourite present is a detective book – I'm loving the story.

-ing forms

G *Page 78*

5 Put the verbs about liking or disliking in the correct column. Then complete the table below with the correct prepositions.

> ~~enjoy~~ like ~~hate~~ don't mind
> quite like can't stand dislike
> love look forward

+ ☺	– ☹
enjoy	hate

good .....*at*.....
afraid ....
interested ....
look forward ....
worried ....
fond ....

6 Complete the sentences with the correct form of the verbs in brackets. Which sentences also need a preposition?

1 I really enjoy .... (go) swimming. It's great fun!
2 I'm not looking forward .... (get) my homework back – I'm sure it was wrong.
3 My brother's interested .... (learn) to fly – he wants to be a pilot.
4 I hate .... (cycle) in the rain – it's awful!
5 I'm quite good .... (make) cakes – I'll make you one!
6 My sister's worried .... (fail) her exams, but I know she'll do well.

READING

Part 5

1 **Choose the correct word to complete the sentences.**

1 *Because / Although* I enjoy school, I look forward to going every day.
2 *If / Unless* I'm ill, I hardly ever miss a day at school.
3 *Despite / If* it's raining, we won't have our sports lesson outside.
4 I bought a ticket for the bus. *However, / So* I decided to go with my friend by bike instead.
5 *Although / Because* I didn't eat much at lunchtime, I wasn't hungry in the afternoon.
6 *Despite / Although* the cold weather, I still wanted to walk home from school.

2 **Complete the sentences with a connecting word from Exercise 1.**

1 .... Peter is going away on holiday, he can't come to the school party.
2 .... we haven't got a gym, our school is really nice.
3 I bought a new calculator for the maths exam. ...., the questions were easy so I didn't use it.
4 .... I'm late for the tennis lesson, please don't wait for me.

Exam task

Read the text below and choose the correct word for each space.
For each question, mark the correct letter **A**, **B**, **C** or **D** on your answer sheet.

School in 15th century England

How different was life for school children in Tudor England, **(0)** .... 400 years ago? The biggest difference is that not many children **(1)** .... had the chance to go to school. Those that went were mainly boys **(2)** .... rich families could afford to pay the fees. Girls were **(3)** .... kept at home to help with housework or sent out to work to **(4)** .... some money. They weren't **(5)** .... to go to school.

At school, boys often had to speak in Latin. There were very few books, so each pupil read from a wooden board **(6)** .... They attended school six days a week, and teachers were very **(7)** .... – boys were punished if they broke the school **(8)** .... When boys left school, they could go to university, with some boys as **(9)** .... as fourteen attending classes. **(10)** ...., at that time there were only two universities – Oxford and Cambridge.

0	(**A**) over	**B**	above	**C**	across	**D**	round
1	**A** even	**B**	never	**C**	just	**D**	only
2	**A** who	**B**	which	**C**	whose	**D**	what
3	**A** neither	**B**	or	**C**	such	**D**	either
4	**A** collect	**B**	bring	**C**	earn	**D**	win
5	**A** approved	**B**	allowed	**C**	agreed	**D**	admitted
6	**A** altogether	**B**	meanwhile	**C**	otherwise	**D**	instead
7	**A** heavy	**B**	strict	**C**	annoyed	**D**	exact
8	**A** rules	**B**	duties	**C**	laws	**D**	orders
9	**A** soon	**B**	small	**C**	early	**D**	young
10	**A** Although	**B**	However	**C**	Despite	**D**	Because

3 **Work in pairs.** Would you like to go to a school like the one in the text? Why? / Why not?

4 From what you have learned from the text, how was life in Tudor England different from life in your country nowadays?

1 WRITING

 W Page 86

Notes & emails

1 Look at the note and answer the questions.

   1 Who is the note to?
   2 Who is it from?

2 Circle two more verbs that describe what the writer is doing in the note.

   persuading   thanking   (apologising)
   explaining   suggesting   warning
   inviting   describing   advising

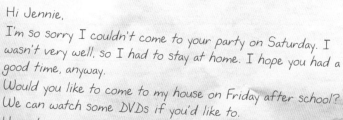

Hi Jennie,
I'm so sorry I couldn't come to your party on Saturday. I wasn't very well, so I had to stay at home. I hope you had a good time, anyway.
Would you like to come to my house on Friday after school? We can watch some DVDs if you'd like to.
Hope to see you then.
Samantha

3 Write the phrases Samantha uses to express the verbs in Exercise 2.

   Apologising..   I'm sorry I couldn't come..
   ....
   ....

4 What is the speaker doing in each sentence? Use the verbs from Exercise 2.

   1 Please help me with my homework! You will? Great!   persuading
   2 It was really kind of you to send me a present on my birthday.   ....
   3 I wouldn't go into town today if I were you – it's really crowded!   ....
   4 My new bicycle's red with silver wheels – it's really fast!   ....
   5 Be careful on your bike! The roads are really slippery!   ....
   6 Let's meet at the shopping centre at 6.00, shall we?   ....
   7 I'm so sorry I was late yesterday.   ....
   8 Would you like to come shopping with me?   ....
   9 I was late because I had to help my mum before I left.   ....

5 Work in pairs. Imagine you have to write two notes. Use the sentences and pictures to decide what you could write in your note. Use the words in brackets to help you.

A I'm sorry I couldn't meet you yesterday but ...

(explain why)

(invite your friend)

B I went shopping yesterday, and I bought ...

(describe your skateboard)

(suggest where to meet)

Linking words

6 Rewrite the sentences using *and, but, so* and *because*.

1 I was tired. I'd played football all day.
I was tired because I'd played football all day.
2 I arrived home. I opened the door.
3 I shouted hello. No one was at home.
4 I was hungry. I made myself a sandwich.
5 My sandwich wasn't very nice. I'd put lots of salt in it.
6 I wanted to make toast. I'd used all the bread.

7 Complete the sentences with a suitable linking word.

1 I didn't feel well .... I went straight to bed when I got home.
2 I got onto my bike .... cycled into town.
3 I have to do my homework tonight .... it's due in tomorrow.
4 I remember putting my mobile into my bag .... now it's not there!
5 .... I didn't have any money, I still went into town.
6 .... the rain, we enjoyed our game of football.

Beginnings & endings

8 Look at the possible ways of starting and finishing emails or notes. Then write a short note to the people below.

Hi Elsa!	See you soon
Dear Jan	Lots of love
Hello Ben	Bye for now
Gina,	Best wishes

1 Explain to your teacher that you will be absent from class.
2 Ask your friend if you can have your sunglasses back.

Punctuation

Exam tip

It's important when you're writing to put in some punctuation. Remember to use full stops and commas. ✓

9 Look at the note Jennie has written to her friend Robyn. Add the missing capital letters, full stops and question marks.

Hi Robyn,
I'm sorry, but I can't come to the cinema tomorrow I have to go to the dentist I'd forgotten all about it until my mum reminded me I don't think I'll be home in time for the film my appointment's at two o'clock and the film starts at three, doesn't it maybe we could go on Saturday instead what do you think let me know see you soon, Jennie

Exam task

You have just bought a new poster to put on the wall of your room.
Write a note to your friend Jan.
In your note, you should:
- tell Jan where you bought the poster
- describe the poster
- suggest when Jan could come and see it.
Write 35–45 words.

Exam tip

Remember to think about who you are writing to and how you will start and finish your note. Don't forget to check that you have included all three points and written the right number of words. ✓

2 Winning & losing
READING Sport

Part 3

1 How many Olympic sports can you name?

2 Write the missing words.

Noun (person)	Noun	Adjective
(1)	championship	–
athlete	(2)	athletic
(3)	competition	(4) ....

3 Complete the sentences with the correct form of a word from Exercise 2.

1 Some of the best ath.................... come from Jamaica.
2 This year the golf champ.................... was in Scotland.
3 You have to be a very comp.................... person to succeed in sport.
4 I don't like sports. I'm not very ath.................... .

Exam task

Look at sentences 1 and 2 below about BMX biking.
Read the first part of the text on page 15 to decide if each sentence is correct or incorrect.
If it is correct, tick **A**. If it is not correct, tick **B**.

1 BMX biking was invented by children. **A** ☐ **B** ☐
2 In the beginning, BMX riders rode their bikes on tracks used by motocross racers. **A** ☐ **B** ☐

> **Exam tip**
>
> When the text is divided into sections, it's sometimes easier to read the first two or three questions and then find the answer by reading the first section of the text. Continue in this way with the other questions. ✓

The History of BMX Biking

How it started

BMX biking began in the late 1960s in southern California. It's based on the sport of motocross, which dates back to 1924 and involves racing motorbikes across rough tracks. It started when children began to copy motocross riders by racing their bikes on tracks which they built themselves. This new form of bike racing was named bicycle motocross, or BMX.

Now do the rest of the task. Decide if each sentence is correct or incorrect.

3 *On Any Sunday* was a film about the first BMX race.
4 The Schwinn Sting-Ray was the favourite model of BMX riders to begin with.
5 More BMX bikes were sold than any other type of bike in the USA in the early 1970s.
6 There were races for different age groups at the first BMX world championships.
7 Boys and girls competed against each other at the first BMX world championships.
8 There were only male BMX competitors at the Beijing Olympics.
9 BMX freestyle started because BMX riders wanted new challenges.
10 Freestyle soon became more popular than racing.

Popularity

In July 1971, a movie about motocross called *On Any Sunday* came out. At the start of the film a group of kids from California are shown riding their bicycles as if they were riding motorbikes. This helped to make BMX biking more popular. Soon BMX races attracted hundreds of riders.

BMX Bikes

In the late 1960s and early 1970s, the most famous BMX bike was the Schwinn Sting-Ray; this was the bike every young rider wanted to own. At this time 70 per cent of all bicycle sales in the USA were either the Sting-Ray or similar models. By the mid 1970s BMX design had improved a lot and there were many new models to choose from. But the bikes all had the same sized wheels and usually only one brake.

World Competition

In 1977, the American Bicycle Association was formed to organise the competitions and to make the rules. The sport was also becoming popular in other parts of the world, particularly in Europe. The first BMX world championship was held in Indianapolis, USA, in 1978. Most of the 165 competitors were teenagers, but there were also children competing in special races for the under 8s and under 12s. There were separate races for boys and girls. There weren't many nationalities present at this competition; apart from Americans there were only a few riders from Australia, Japan and Venezuela.

Since that time the number of races for adults has grown very quickly, but BMX racing didn't become a full Olympic sport until the 2008 Summer Olympics in Beijing. Maris Stromberg from Latvia won the first ever Olympic men's gold medal for BMX racing and Anne-Caroline Chausson from France became the first women's champion.

Freestyle

As the popularity of BMX grew, riders were constantly testing the limits of their bikes. BMX wasn't just about racing any more. Riders began to take their bikes to skateboard parks and started performing tricks and jumps. This became known as 'freestyle' and riders soon began to practise this as much as racing.

4 Work in pairs. Discuss these questions.

1 How popular is BMX biking where you live?
2 How are BMX bikes different from other bikes?
3 Have you ever tried / Would you like to try BMX racing?

GRAMMAR

Past simple

 Page 79

1 Look at the text about BMX biking on page 15 again.

  1 <u>Underline</u> two examples of regular past simple verbs in the text.
  2 Circle two examples of irregular past simple verbs.
  3 Find an example of the negative past simple form of *be*.
  4 Find an example of a negative past simple form with another verb.

2 Choose the correct verb form.

  1 The boys didn't *like / liked* the new football shirts.
  2 We *was / were* very happy when we won the match.
  3 Snowboarding *became / become* an Olympic winter sport in 1998.
  4 Brazil first *won / did win* the World Cup in 1958.

3 Complete the sentences with the correct past simple form of the verbs in brackets.

  1 Layla and Brooke both .... (play) for the school basketball team last year.
  2 Max .... (not learn) to ride a bike until he was eight.
  3 Jay .... (win) the diving competition.
  4 Where .... (Lauren / buy) her tennis racket?
  5 .... (be) the ticket for the match expensive?
  6 There .... (not be) enough players to have a game of football.

Past continuous

 Page 79

4 Look at the past continuous sentences below. Which sentence describes:

  a an interrupted action?
  b something that happened over a period of time?
  c an incomplete action happening at a moment in time?

  1 BMX biking was becoming popular in other parts of the world.
  2 While my brother was racing down the hill, he fell off his bike and broke his leg.
  3 At 6.00 p.m. yesterday I was walking home from the park.

5 Choose the correct verb form, past simple or past continuous.

  1 *Did you go / Were you going* shopping when I *saw / was seeing* you on the train yesterday?
  2 We *were winning / won* by two goals and then the other team *was scoring / scored* three goals in the last ten minutes.

6 Work in pairs. Ask and answer questions about what you were doing yesterday.

  shower / 7.00 a.m.?
  breakfast / 8.30 a.m.?
  study maths / 10.30 a.m.?
  lunch / 12.30 p.m.?

> Were you having a shower at 7.00 a.m.?

> No. I was sleeping.

2 LISTENING

Part 3

1 🔊 **08** Listen to the recording. Tick (✔) the number you hear.

1	13th March ☐	30th March ☐	**4**	250 ☐	2,500 ☐		
2	£1.50 ☐	£1.15 ☐	**5**	2011 ☐	2001 ☐		
3	1998 ☐	1988 ☐					

2 🔊 **09** Listen and complete the text with the correct numbers.

Tyler Wright

Born on **(1)** .... 1994 in Australia
Won her first adult competition at the age of **(2)** ....
The prize money for this competition was **(3)** $..........
Became under-18 champion in **(4)** ....
In 2011 she won the women's World Cup, scoring just over
(5) .... points out of 20

Exam tips

In this part of the Test, you often have to listen for and write down numbers. This can be a date, time or price.

Before you listen, try and identify what kind of information is missing – a number, a name or another noun. ✔

3 Work in pairs. Discuss these questions.

1 Which of these things do you think is most important to become a sports champion?

> talent   money   family help   good teachers   luck   ambition

2 Do you think it's more difficult to be a champion footballer, ice skater, BMX racer or surfer?

Exam task

🔊 **10** You will hear a man called Don Wood talking about a special sports school on the radio.

For each question, fill in the missing information in the numbered space.

International Sports Academy (ISA)

For students aged **(0)** ...... 12–18 ......

Interviews

The interviews for new students are on **(1)** ....

To arrange an interview call Leo **(2)** .... on 0998 354678.

Programme

Students choose one main sport (ISA are offering **(3)** .... as a new sport).

Students must do sports training and **(4)** .... each week after school.

To perform well in competitions, students must also learn to train their **(5)** ....

The personal coach helps students with organising their **(6)** ....

4 Work in pairs. Discuss these questions.

1 Would you like to go to a special sports school like ISA? Why? / Why not?
2 What sports lessons do you have at school? What do you like or dislike about them?
3 How old were you when you learned to swim / ride a bicycle / ...?

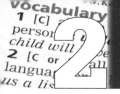

VOCABULARY

1 Complete the sentences with the correct form of these phrasal verbs.

believe in   get in   ~~hand in~~   give in   join in   stay in

1 I mustn't forget to ....*hand in*.... my homework tomorrow.
2 Harry always knew he would be a champion. He always .... himself.
3 She never wants to .... with any team games.
4 We arrived late and the gates were locked, so we couldn't .... to see the match.
5 Ali's not coming out this evening. He's ....
6 Real champions never .... They fight to the end.

2 Match the words and phrases (1–10) with A or B.

A A bad loser ...
B A good loser ...

1 is polite
2 is rude
3 has a positive attitude
4 has a negative attitude
5 shows respect for their opponent
6 shows a lack of respect for their opponent
7 often bursts into tears
8 never bursts into tears
9 shows their disappointment
10 hides their disappointment

3 Choose the best verb to complete the sentences.

1 She *beat / won* her 100m record by 0.2 seconds.
2 We *won / defeated* our match by two goals.
3 They *lost / failed* to reach the final of the competition.
4 The other team didn't *defeat / defend* us because we wanted to win more than they did.
5 You can *achieve / succeed* your dreams if you work hard enough.
6 He *succeeded / achieved* in beating the defending champion.

2 READING | Hobbies & leisure

Part 5

1 Cross out the verb which you <u>cannot</u> use with the nouns in bold.

1 It's a good idea to work out so you can *stay / get / reach* **fit and healthy**.
2 It's important to *feel / show / make* **respect** for yourself.
3 It can take a long time to *enjoy / bring / have* **success**.
4 You shouldn't give up too easily and *admit / ask / accept* **defeat**.

Exam task

Read the text below and choose the correct word for each space.

For each question, mark the correct letter **A**, **B**, **C** or **D** on your answer sheet.

The importance of team games

Taking part in games and sports teaches young people a lot of very useful skills as well as helping them to **(0)** .... fit and healthy. Firstly, games which involve more than just a contest **(1)** .... two competitors teach people to **(2)** .... respect for the law because no game will work unless **(3)** .... plays according to the rules.

The other thing you discover is that you cannot **(4)** .... success by yourself in a team game. You have to **(5)** .... each other, otherwise you can never win.

(6) .... team games also teaches you that losing isn't the end of the world. There's always **(7)** .... opportunity and you may be more **(8)** .... against your opponents next time. It is essential to learn how to be a good loser **(9)** .... being able to **(10)** .... defeat is an important lesson in life.

> **Exam tip**
>
> Read the whole sentence. Look at the words that come immediately before and after the missing word to make sure the word you choose fits into the sentence. ✓

0 **A** keep	**B** increase	**C** grow	**D** come
1 **A** on	**B** between	**C** from	**D** about
2 **A** get	**B** be	**C** have	**D** give
3 **A** everyone	**B** all	**C** anyone	**D** most
4 **A** know	**B** reach	**C** bring	**D** achieve
5 **A** share	**B** support	**C** work	**D** participate
6 **A** Letting	**B** Making	**C** Taking	**D** Playing
7 **A** another	**B** some	**C** much	**D** any
8 **A** strong	**B** successful	**C** lucky	**D** hopeful
9 **A** or	**B** but	**C** because	**D** although
10 **A** meet	**B** face	**C** try	**D** lose

2 WRITING

Part 3

Page 88

1 Look at this Writing Part 3 task. Would you choose the letter or the story? Why?

Write an answer to one of the questions (7 or 8) in this part.

Write your answer in about 100 words on your answer sheet.

Mark the question number in the box at the top of your answer sheet.

....

Question 7

- This is part of a letter you receive from an English friend.

> I play hockey at a club every Saturday. Last week we won for the first time! Tell me about a sport that you do. Where do you play? What do you enjoy about it? Who do you play with?

- Now write a letter to your friend.
- Write your **letter** on your answer sheet.

Question 8

- Your English teacher has asked you to write a story.
- Your story must begin with this sentence:

> When I woke up I was very nervous because I wanted to win the competition so much.

- Write your **story** on your answer sheet.

---

2 Look at the letter in Exercise 3 that an exam candidate wrote for Question 7. Discuss the questions in pairs.

Does Frankie

1 answer all the questions in the task?
2 include a variety of tenses?
3 include any linking words?
4 include any adjectives?
5 use an appropriate way to start / finish the letter?
6 write the correct number of words?
7 organise ideas into paragraphs?

3 Look at the notes the teacher made. Can you correct Frankie's mistakes?

Dear George,

Last week I went to my new club for the first time. It was **(1)** <u>very funny</u> there. *(wrong adjective)* We played soccer and won the game against another town. First we thought that we would lose, but I **(2)** <u>made</u> the *(wrong verb)* final point. I met some new people there. They **(3)** <u>was</u> very friendly. After *(wrong agreement)* the game we went to a restaurant and ate together. We spoke about a special event we want to have next week. It should be a very big party in the soccer-club. I hope that it will be good. Write back soon.

Frankie

4 Now plan the story in Question 8. Which of the following pieces of information do you think you could include?

- why you wanted to win the competition
- a description of what you ate for breakfast
- what kind of competition it was
- what happened in the competition
- how you felt about winning / losing
- what the prize was

Exam task

Write your story.

> **Exam tip**
>
> Try to end your story in an interesting way. ✓

2 SPEAKING

Part 2

1 Put these phrases for agreeing and disagreeing under the correct heading.

> You're right.
> That's true.
> I'm not sure about that.
> You're wrong.
> I think so too.
> Yes, but don't you think ...?
> I suppose so.

Agreeing	Disagreeing

2 🔘 11 Listen and decide which student you agree with, Lina or Max. Tick (✔) the expressions in Exercise 1 you hear.

3 Work in pairs. Agree or disagree with these statements. Say why you agree or disagree.

> Argentina is the best football team in the world.

> We should have longer summer holidays.

> Everyone should play in a sports team.

Exam task

🔘 12 Listen to the examiner and do the task.

Exam tip

Listen carefully to your partner's opinions and use phrases for agreeing and disagreeing. ✓

3 Let's shop!

LISTENING | Clothes

1 Work in pairs. Describe these clothes.

2 Put the items below into the correct categories. Two words can go in two categories.

Clothes and shoes   **Jewellery**

jacket
leather   pink   necklace   top
plain   sandals   trainers   suit   stripes
spots   light blue   gold   cream   sweatshirt
dark green   gloves   silk   cotton   purple   silver
wool   navy blue   earrings   skirt
shirt   bracelet   jeans
dress   ring

Colours and patterns   **Materials**

G *Page 80*

3 🔘 **13** Listen to Marcia talking about a shopping trip with a friend. Tick (✔) the things Marcia liked.

the department store ☐   the purple T-shirt with silver stars ☐

the black cotton jeans ☐   the silver bracelet ☐

the navy blue sandals ☐

4 Read the multiple-choice questions below, then listen again. While you are listening, choose the correct answer, A, B or C.

1 What did Marcia and her friend buy in the department store?
   A trousers and jewellery
   B trousers and a top
   C a top and jewellery

2 What did Marcia think of the shoe shop they went to?
   A It was too small.
   B It had a limited range of goods.
   C Its prices were all too high.

Exam task

> **Exam tip**
>
> The questions on the recording may be very similar to the ones on your page. Follow each one carefully so that you don't get lost while you're listening – the questions are in the same order as the recording. ✓

🔘 **14** You will hear an interview with two young teenagers, Ben Wright and Sophie Carter, who design and make their own clothes. For each question, choose the correct answer A, B or C.

1 What made Ben decide to start designing his own T-shirts?
   A a present he received
   B a TV programme
   C something he saw on the internet

2 Ben put his designs onto his T-shirts by
   A using an iron.
   B sewing them.
   C drawing them on.

3 When Ben's friends saw his T-shirts, they
   A asked Ben to design one for them.
   B wanted to make one of their own.
   C put a photo of one in the school magazine.

4 Who helps out in Sophie's after-school class?
   A some older students
   B other teachers from the school
   C parents of the people attending

5 Sophie thinks the class is popular with students because
   A they end up with really unusual clothes.
   B they save money by making their own clothes.
   C they can show other students what they've done.

6 What does Sophie want to improve?
   A her sewing skills for making her designs
   B her choices of suitable colours and materials
   C her drawings for her designs

3 SPEAKING

Part 4

1 Work in pairs. Look at the teenagers in the two photos, and describe what they are wearing. What's your opinion of how they look? ⟶ *Page 124*

2 Look at what different people say about where they get the clothes they wear.

My family often gives me clothes as presents.

I borrow my older sister's things – they're always really cool!

I buy clothes when I'm in town with friends.

My parents take me on shopping trips to buy them.

My mum orders them for me online.

I go to the small shops in my town – I don't like big stores!

Where do you get *your* clothes from? Talk with your partner.

3 🔘 **15** You are going to hear two friends, Rolph and Karina, talking about what they do in town with their friends. Listen and complete the conversation.

Karina: So what do you (1) .... in town with friends, Rolph? Do you (2) .... go shopping?

Rolph: Sometimes, if I've got enough money. (3) .... ?

Karina: We go quite often, but it's expensive, (4) .... ?

Rolph: (5) .... – clothes cost a lot for students, (6) .... ?

Karina: (7) .... , so we (8) .... looking round the shops. (9) .... you (10) .... ?

Rolph: Well, if we haven't got any money, we (11) .... to a café or plan trips to the sports centre. Shopping's boring if you can't buy anything.

Karina: (12) .... ? I'm (13) .... about that.

Exam task

> **Exam tip**
> Listen to what your partner says to find things that you can ask questions about. Keep the conversation going with questions using *Why, When, What, What kind of.* ✓

⟶ *Page 125*

Read the exam task below, then close your books and talk together.

> Your photographs show **different places to shop**. Talk together about **where** you like to go to buy things and **who** you like to go with.

> **Exam tip**
> Part 4 lasts about three minutes. You need to take turns talking and show interest in what your partner is saying. ✓

GRAMMAR Shopping

Comparing

G *Page 80*

1 Think about your favourite shop. How would you describe it? Think about these things.

> what it sells   the prices   the size
> the staff – are they helpful?
> Does it have the best clothes in the town?
> Is it the cheapest / the most expensive / the biggest shop?

2 Work in pairs. Talk about the shop you chose in Exercise 1. Try to give reasons for your answers.

> For me it has the best clothes in town, because although I'm tall, they still fit me really well.

3 Complete the table.

cheap	cheaper	the cheapest
expensive	more expensive	the most expensive
fashionable		
interesting		
big		
comfortable		
good		
bad		

4 🔘 **16** Listen to a boy called Steven comparing two big shops, Denhams and Bryants, in his city. Which one is better for each of the things he mentions below? Tick (✔) the correct shop.

5 Complete the sentences using information from the table in Exercise 4 to help you.

1 Clothes in Bryants are .... than the ones in Denhams.
2 There are .... sizes available in Denhams .... in Bryants.
3 The clothes in Denhams are not .... fashionable .... the ones in Bryants.
4 The changing rooms in Bryants are .... than those in Denhams.
5 Denhams has .... sports clothes .... Bryants.
6 The food in the café at Bryants is not .... nice .... the food at Denhams.

6 🔘 **17** Listen to Steven talking about another shop, called Cavenhams. Complete the sentences.

1 Cavenhams has .... books in the city.
2 The milkshakes at Cavenhams are .... anywhere!

7 Compare your favourite shop with another shop in the town. Which one is bigger / nicer / more expensive? Which one sells better things?

	Denhams	Bryants
cheap	☐	☐
big sizes available	☐	☐
fashionable clothes	☐	☐
comfortable changing rooms	☐	☐
good sports clothes	☐	☐
nice food in the café	☐	☐

3 READING

Part 5

Exam task

Read the text below and choose the correct word for each space.
For each question, mark the correct letter **A**, **B**, **C** or **D** on your answer sheet.

Harrods

Harrods department store in London is **(0)** .... biggest shop in the UK. It started as a small fruit and vegetable shop **(1)** .... a small number of staff, but it has **(2)** .... into a store with several levels, hundreds of departments and thousands of staff. There are lots of restaurants inside, so regular customers could **(3)** .... up having lunch in a different one every day for a month **(4)** .... they wished!

(5) .... above the store are the words 'All Things for all People, Anywhere', as the shop says that customers can buy **(6)** .... anything from Harrods. Up **(7)** .... the 1960s, you could even buy a baby lion from its pet department!

At night, Harrods store front is lit up with more lights **(8)** .... any other store in London – 12,000 lights in total. Also, the store has its own private water supply from three holes in the **(9)** ...., one of which is almost 500 feet **(10)** .... ! Harrods is really full of surprises!

0	**Ⓐ** the	**B**	any	**C**	one	**D**	a
1	**A** working	**B**	employing	**C**	using	**D**	handling
2	**A** increased	**B**	become	**C**	improved	**D**	developed
3	**A** put	**B**	go	**C**	end	**D**	keep
4	**A** if	**B**	whether	**C**	although	**D**	unless
5	**A** Added	**B**	Built	**C**	Written	**D**	Created
6	**A** definitely	**B**	absolutely	**C**	perfectly	**D**	totally
7	**A** from	**B**	since	**C**	during	**D**	until
8	**A** than	**B**	for	**C**	as	**D**	like
9	**A** floor	**B**	ground	**C**	land	**D**	space
10	**A** far	**B**	low	**C**	deep	**D**	long

3 READING

1 Do the questionnaire about shopping in town. Then compare your answers with a partner.

Shopping in town

How often do you go shopping in town? (Tick a box)

☐ every day ☐ once a week ☐ once a fortnight ☐ once a month ☐ whenever I have time

How do you get to town?

☐ by bus ☐ by train ☐ by car ☐ by bicycle ☐ on foot

Who do you go into town with?

☐ my parents ☐ my grandparents ☐ my brother and sisters ☐ my friends ☐ by myself

Which places do you go to while you're in town?

☐ bus station ☐ department stores ☐ small shops ☐ music shops ☐ bookshops ☐ clothes shops
☐ sports shops ☐ park ☐ café ☐ fast-food restaurant ☐ cinema ☐ train station

2 What signs and notices might you see during a shopping trip in town? Where might you see them?

3 Look at the signs and notices below. Write the correct letter next to each place.

A
Customers are requested to queue here to pay for items

B
Please note – drinks and food are forbidden inside this store.

C
Buses depart from here every ten minutes

D
Rail Services
We regret to inform passengers that the 15.30 to London has been delayed

E
Customers – please clear your tables before leaving

F
You may try on two items only at a time

G
Two tickets for the price of one on films showing before 2.30 p.m.

Places

on a shop door	....B....
at a cash desk	....
inside a fast-food restaurant	....
at a bus stop	....
inside a changing room	....
on a station platform	....
at a cinema	....

Exam tip

The language used in the signs and notices that you may see in the test can be more formal than in the notes and messages. ✓

4 Match the formal words from the signs and notices in Exercise 3 with the correct meaning.

1 depart   a late
2 request   b tell
3 forbidden   c feel sorry
4 regret   d ask
5 delayed   e leave
6 inform   f not allowed

5 Read the email opposite and answer the questions.

1 Who is the email to?
2 Who is it from?
3 Who are Jane, Maria and Sophie, do you think?
4 What is the email about?
5 What examples of informal language are in the email?
6 Which of these functions is the writer doing?

asking for a suggestion, changing something, giving information, cancelling something, thanking someone

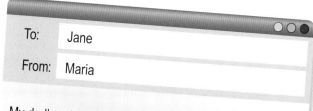

To: Jane

From: Maria

My dad's said he'll drive us into town on Saturday to go shopping, so we'll pick you up at 11 a.m., OK? We need to get a present for Sophie – any ideas?

6 Now look at a Reading Part 1 question about the email. Which is the correct answer, A, B or C?

Maria wants to
A make a suggestion to Jane about what gift to buy for Sophie.
B tell Jane about the travel arrangements for the weekend.
C check that Jane still wants to go shopping in town.

Exam task

Look at the text in each question. What does it say? Mark the correct letter **A**, **B** or **C** on your answer sheet.

Exam tip

Decide what the function is in each text before you look at the A, B and C options. This helps you to understand the purpose of the text. ✓

1

We do not give refunds for reduced items you have bought in our sale

2

Hi Sam,
I'm in a café with Dan. We're going into Railtons store shortly to choose some football kit. Come and join us! We'll be here till 3 p.m. Jake

3

To: **All students**

From: Mrs Matthews

We have just had a delivery of new school sweatshirts. Students wishing to buy one to wear should come to the office at lunchtime.

4

No more than **three** items allowed in changing rooms at any time.

5

Hi Dan,

My brother won't let me borrow his baseball boots, so I need to buy some. Can you tell me which shop in town you bought yours from? Thanks. Harry

1 A There are no reduced items on sale in the store at the moment.
  B You can't get money back for things you got cheaply in the sale.
  C Refunds for reduced items cannot be given after the sale has finished.

2 A Sam can meet Jake and Dan at the café if he goes before 3 p.m.
  B Jake wants Sam to help him choose new sports clothes.
  C Dan and Jake will wait for Sam to arrive before they go to Railtons.

3 A Some new school uniform is available in the office.
  B Students must wear their new school sweatshirts during the lunch break today.
  C The office is expecting items of new school clothing to be delivered at lunchtime.

4 A You cannot try on items anywhere except in the changing rooms.
  B You may take a maximum of three items with you into the changing rooms.
  C There are only three changing rooms available at any time for trying on items.

5 Harry wants to
  A meet Dan in town to borrow his baseball boots.
  B tell Dan which shop he can get some baseball boots from.
  C find out where Dan went to get his baseball boots.

3 WRITING

W Page 88

Exam tip

Check through pieces of writing that you get back from your teacher. Do you always make the same mistakes? Keep a list so that you remember what to look for when you're checking your work. ✓

1 Work in pairs. Look at the photos. How would you describe the way the people are dressed? Use these words.

| traditional   smart   casual   fashionable   stylish   comfortable |

2 Discuss these questions.

1 How would you describe the way you and your friends dress?
2 What's the latest fashion in clothes in your country right now?

3 Work in pairs. Read what Monika says about young people in her city. Is it the same where you live?

Young people in my city like wearing clothes in bright colours, with lots of different patterns on **them**. Denim shorts and jackets are really popular, and T-shirts too. **They** often have the name of the store written across the front. But no one seems to wear big T-shirts and loose jeans any more, like my brother and his friends always wore for skateboarding. **He** never wore anything else!

Exam tip

Pronouns are useful because they help you to avoid repeating the same words. ✓

4 Look at the pronouns in bold that Monika uses. Answer the questions.

1 What does **them** refer to?
   a clothes   b bright colours
2 What does **They** refer to?
   a denim shorts   b T-shirts
3 What does **He** refer to?
   a Monika's brother b her brother's friends

5 Replace the underlined words in the text with these pronouns.

| she   them   it   ~~her~~   they   there |
| his   that   we   he   us |

Whenever I go somewhere special, I ask my older sister if I can borrow (1) ~~my~~ *her* ~~older sister's~~ clothes. (2) My older sister doesn't mind if I borrow (3) the clothes, which is lucky – and (4) the clothes fit me perfectly! I also go shopping in my favourite shop, where I can get things like jewellery cheaply. (5) My favourite shop isn't far from my home, so my dad usually drives me (6) to my favourite shop in (7) my dad's car, and then (8) my dad leaves me to meet my friends, who love shopping in town, too – when (9) my friends and I have money to spend. But (10) having some money to spend usually only happens if our parents give (11) my friends and me some!

6 Read the text in Exercise 5 again. <u>Underline</u> examples of *which*, *where* and *who*.

7 Look at sentences a–c. Then rewrite sentences 1–6 using *who*, *which* or *where*.

   a I've got a good friend called Isabelle. She loves buying clothes.
   *I've got a good friend called Isabelle **who** loves buying clothes.*

   b She often goes to a big shop in town. She can buy great clothes cheaply there.
   *She often goes to a big shop in town **where** she can buy great clothes cheaply.*

   c She found a wonderful costume last week. It was perfect for our school party.
   *She found a wonderful costume last week **which** was perfect for our school fancy dress party.*

   1 I go to a small shop near the market. You can buy great clothes there.

   2 I bought a really pretty dress. It was quite like one of Isabelle's.

   3 I showed the dress to Isabelle. She thought it suited me.

   4 My sister liked my dress too. That was a surprise.

   5 Then yesterday I saw one of my classmates. She was wearing the same dress!

   6 Next week we're going shopping together. It will be fun.

8 ⊙ Exam candidates often make mistakes with pronouns. Cross out the incorrect pronoun in each sentence.

   1 I don't often find clothes *who* / *which* fit me well.

   2 He was escaping from the police *who* / *which* were looking for him.

   3 I like reading magazines *who* / *which* are about music.

   4 The programme is about two brothers *which* / *who* were born in Brazil.

   5 I have a friend called Sol *who* / *which* is twelve years old, like me.

   6 I really like reading magazines *which* / *who* talk about cars.

   7 The countryside is more peaceful and relaxing than the city, *who* / *which* is noisier and more polluted.

   8 We are a school *which* / *who* always keeps the environment clean.

 Page 80

Exam task

Write an answer to one of the questions (1 or 2) in this part.
Write your answer in about 100 words on your answer sheet.

Question 1

- This is part of a letter you receive from your English friend Becky.

> I'm doing a school project on what teenagers really like wearing – including their school uniforms! What sort of clothes do *you* like wearing? And do you like or dislike school uniforms? Why?

- Now write a letter to Becky, answering her questions.
- Write your **letter** on your answer sheet.

Question 2

- Your English teacher has asked you to write a story.
- Your story must begin with this sentence:
  Sarah was excited about her fantastic costume as she set off to the party.
- Write your **story** on your answer sheet.

4 Relax!
READING Personal feelings

Part 4

1 Write the name of three films you enjoyed in the table.
   Then find one student who liked each film, and one
   student who didn't.

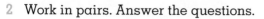

Film	Name (☺)	Name (☹)
Science fiction:		
Scary movie:		
Comedy:		

2 Work in pairs. Answer the questions.

   1 Do you prefer watching films on TV or at the cinema?
   2 What is your favourite film? Why do you like it?

3 Think of some facts, opinions and feelings about your favourite film. Then tell
   your partner about it.

   Fact   **Opinion**   **Feeling**

   It's about a horse.   It's interesting and very sad.   It makes me cry.

4 Look at questions 1–5 in the exam task on page 31. Are they testing understanding
   of fact, opinion or feeling?

Exam task

Read the text and questions below.
For each question, choose the correct letter, **A**, **B**, **C** or **D**.

My favourite movies
by Sean Heston

I've always loved scary movies. I remember the first one I watched very
clearly. My dad's favourite films were his DVD collection of old black
and white thrillers. One day while my parents were out, I decided to
watch one of these DVDs on my laptop.

The quality wasn't great because the screen was very small and I
wasn't used to watching black and white films. I felt guilty because I
hadn't asked my parents' permission to watch the film, but excited at
the same time. I was also anxious in case it would be too frightening.
Luckily it wasn't. It was only a little scary and I thought it was brilliant.

After that, from the age of 14–18, I watched all kinds of scary movies with my friends. Films about sharks,
monsters, vampires and ghosts; we loved them all. Sometimes I was so scared I couldn't even look at the
screen and spent most of the time with a cushion over my face. I became too nervous to swim in the sea and
imagined all kinds of creatures hiding in the dark outside my bedroom window.

Since that time, I've watched all these films again and again. I still think they're terrific and they still make me
jump. But I've never been able to explain this strange attraction to fear. How can being frightened be a form
of entertainment for so many people? Is it a way of learning to deal with fear or is it just a way to escape from
boring reality? I have no idea. But what I do know is that I can't live without the excitement of scary movies.

1 In this text Sean is describing
   A what kind of scary movies he prefers.
   B how he changed as a person by watching scary movies.
   C what he liked about his first scary movie.
   D some of his experiences of watching scary movies.

2 How did Sean feel about his first scary movie?
   A He was disappointed because it wasn't very frightening.
   B He had a mix of negative and positive feelings.
   C He was certain he would enjoy it.
   D He couldn't wait to know what happened in the end.

3 What does Sean say about the effect scary movies had on him?
   A He spent too much time watching these films with his friends.
   B They scared him a lot because he was too young to watch them.
   C They changed his attitude to ordinary situations.
   D He wasn't frightened when he was with his friends.

4 What does Sean say about his attraction to fear?
   A He thinks it is something everyone experiences.
   B He believes this has taught him a lot about himself.
   C He is worried it may not be good for him.
   D He doesn't understand why he enjoys being scared.

5 What advice might Sean give to young people about watching scary movies?

A You should never watch scary films alone or without your parents' permission.

B If you are afraid of sharks or ghosts, it's not a good idea to watch certain films.

C Watching scary movies can be a fun thing to do with friends.

D Old movies aren't as frightening as modern ones, so it's good to start with these.

5 Underline two adjectives in the text on page 30 with a similar meaning to each of these words.

worried   fantastic

6 Find these adjectives in the text. Do they refer to a) a feeling b) an opinion?

excited   frightening   scared
boring   frightened

7 Choose the correct adjective and complete the statements so they are true about you. Then compare with a partner. Do you feel the same way as each other?

   1 I get *frightened* / *frightening* when
      ....
   2 I think stories about ....
      .... are very *worried* / *worrying*.
   3 The most *exciting* / *excited* film I've
      ever seen was ....
      ....

8 Work in pairs. Recommend a film to watch with friends at home. Use these phrases.

You should watch ...
I think you would enjoy it because ...

4 GRAMMAR

Present perfect

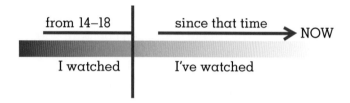

G *Page 81*

1 Look at the examples of sentences using the past simple and the present perfect. Complete the rules with *present perfect* or *past simple*.

*From the age of 14–18, I **watched** all kinds of scary movies with my friends.*
*Since that time I**'ve watched** all these films again and again.*

```
from 14–18        │  since that time
                  │ ─────────────────► NOW
─────────────────────────────────────────
     I watched    │   I've watched
```

1 The .... is used to refer to something that has finished.
2 The .... is used to refer to something that started in the past and is still true now.

2 Look at the examples of other uses of the present perfect. Choose the correct phrases in the explanations.

1 *The news **has finished**. You can watch your programme now.*
  • describes something which happened *very recently / a long time ago*.
2 *I**'ve seen** all the Harry Potter films lots of times.*
  • describes something that happened in the past but the time when it happened *is / is not* given.

3 Complete the sentences with *has, have, has not* or *have not*. In which sentences would it be more natural to use contractions (*'s/'ve/hasn't/haven't*)?

1 .... you ever seen *Star Wars*?
2 My mother .... never watched a scary movie.
3 We .... been to see the new vampire movie. It was great!
4 My teacher .... told us to watch a film in English for homework. I'm going to watch *Toy Story*.
5 My brother .... bought a new DVD for months. He usually buys one every month.
6 I'm so sorry. I .... given you the money for the tickets.

4 Complete the sentences so that they are true for you.

1 I've lived in my house / flat for ....
2 I've studied English since ....
3 I haven't eaten anything for ....
4 I haven't been to the cinema since ....
5 I've known my best friend since ....
6 I haven't bought a new book for ....

5 ⊙ Exam candidates often make mistakes with the present perfect. Choose the correct verb form in these sentences.

1 We *are / have been* friends since that day and we are going to be friends for ever.
2 We *won / have won* the final match last weekend.
3 I *read / have read* your letter ten minutes ago, and I decided to write to you as quickly as possible.
4 Today I will tell you about the new restaurant that *has / had* recently opened in my town.
5 I *was / have been* here since last Monday and the weather has been good.

6 Put the words in the correct order to make questions. Then ask and answer with a partner.

1 watched / DVD / many / How / films / you / have / on / week / this ?
2 this / cinema / How / you / been / times / have / the / to / month / many ?
3 language / in / ever / you / Have / a / seen / film / another ?
4 film / seen / more / times / five / than / you / Which / have ?
5 cried / ever / you / in / movie / a / Have ?
6 scariest / seen / ever / What's / you / the / film / have ?

4 READING

1 Put these adjectives under the correct preposition. Sometimes more than one preposition is possible.

> jealous disappointed afraid annoyed surprised
> satisfied worried excited serious anxious

of	about	by	with

2 Work in pairs. Discuss these questions.

1 Have you ever been jealous of anyone?
2 Have you been excited about anything recently?
3 Have you been annoyed by anyone or anything recently?

> **Exam tip**
>
> Some words in the options may have a similar meaning, but do not fit in the space because they may be followed by a different preposition. ✓

Exam task

Read the text below and choose the correct word for each space.
For each question, mark the correct letter **A**, **B**, **C** or **D** on your answer sheet.

Learning to rock

The Farley Rock School teaches guitar, piano and drums to kids who (0) .... about being a rock star. (1) .... it opened in 2006, over 250 kids aged between 11 and 15 (2) .... experienced the excitement of performing (3) .... stage.

Each week students have a private lesson and also do band practice with other students. At the end of each term, there is a concert for friends and family. Students who have (4) .... a higher level have the (5) .... to perform at local venues such as The Music Factory and Billy's Jazz Club.

'Students (6) .... a lot of progress with us because they are so (7) .... about being in a band,' says Dave Farley, the school's director. 'Even beginners who have (8) .... played in a band before and are (9) .... of performing in public, soon (10) .... confident enough to play in front of hundreds of people. It's amazing.'

0	**A** want	**B** dream	**C** expect	**D** wish
1	**A** Since	**B** After	**C** Before	**D** For
2	**A** must	**B** are	**C** can	**D** have
3	**A** in	**B** on	**C** at	**D** up
4	**A** reached	**B** risen	**C** succeeded	**D** jumped
5	**A** choice	**B** hope	**C** idea	**D** opportunity
6	**A** make	**B** do	**C** get	**D** be
7	**A** keen	**B** excited	**C** determined	**D** interested
8	**A** ever	**B** never	**C** still	**D** yet
9	**A** worried	**B** afraid	**C** anxious	**D** upset
10	**A** improve	**B** develop	**C** become	**D** turn

3 Do you think anyone can be in a rock band? What instrument would you like to learn?

Part 1

1 Look at the pictures for questions 1–7 in the Exam task. Can you name all the things in the pictures? Practise saying the numbers.

2 Look at the questions in the Exam task. <u>Underline</u> the key words.

Exam task

18 For each question choose the correct answer **A**, **B** or **C**.

1 What time does the film start?

A   B   C

5 Which circus tickets did the man decide to buy?

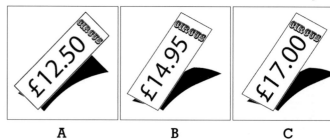

A   B   C

2 What did Jenny buy at the film festival?

A   B   C

6 What do the speakers decide to watch on TV?

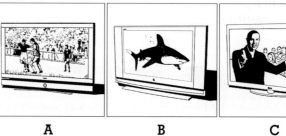

A   B   C

3 Which instrument has the boy recently started learning?

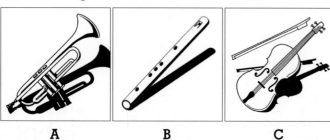

A   B   C

7 Who do the speakers think will win the singing competition?

A   B   C

4 How did the family travel to the concert?

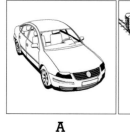

A   B   C

4 SPEAKING

Part 3

1 **19** Listen to Marco describing the people in the photo below. What is he describing?

   A their clothes
   B their appearance
   C their actions

2 What does Marco say when he doesn't know a word?

3 Complete Marco's sentences.

   1 The people .... very excited.
   2 It .... a special day

4 Choose the correct form of the verb.

   1 In this picture I *can see* / *am seeing* ...
   2 In this photo there *is* / *are* a family ...
   3 The woman in the photo *plays* / *is playing* the guitar.
   4 I think this photo *is* / *was* taken in India.
   5 There are some people who *walk* / *are walking* in the park.
   6 The man *wears* / *is wearing* shorts.
   7 I think the woman *is* / *looks* a teacher.
   8 It *looks* / *is looking* like a very peaceful place.

Exam task

Work in pairs. Describe what you can see in the photo. Use the language in Exercises 2–4.

Student A: Describe the people – how they're feeling, their clothes, their age, what they're doing.

Student B: Describe the place – what kind of place it is, which country it could be, what the weather is like .

WRITING

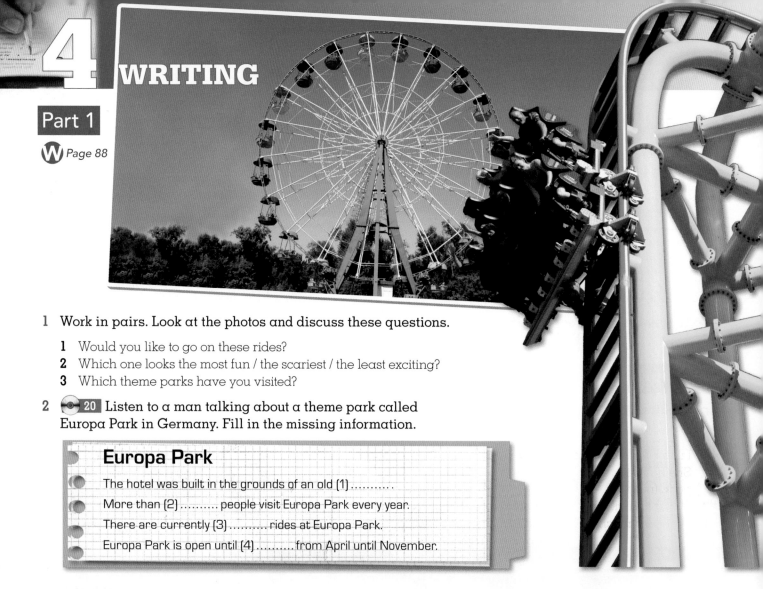

1 Work in pairs. Look at the photos and discuss these questions.

   1 Would you like to go on these rides?
   2 Which one looks the most fun / the scariest / the least exciting?
   3 Which theme parks have you visited?

2 🔘 **20** Listen to a man talking about a theme park called Europa Park in Germany. Fill in the missing information.

> ## Europa Park
>
> The hotel was built in the grounds of an old (1) ....
>
> More than (2) .... people visit Europa Park every year.
>
> There are currently (3) .... rides at Europa Park.
>
> Europa Park is open until (4) .... from April until November.

just / yet / already

Ⓖ *Page 81*

3 Complete sentences 1–3 with *just, yet* or *already*. Then match the sentences with statements a–d.

   1 Europa Park has .... opened a new hotel. It only opened last week.
   2 200,000 people have .... visited Europa Park this year.
   3 The owners of Europa Park haven't finished building all the rides ....

   a This word is used to emphasise that something happened very recently.
   b This word is used to emphasise that something has happened sooner than expected.
   c This word shows the speaker intends to do something.
   d This word is only used in negative statements and questions.

4 Complete the sentences with these words.

> already   for   just   never   since   yet

   1 Jack hasn't been to Europa Park ...., but he really wants to go there.
   2 Amy has .... been to Europa Park. She went last year.
   3 Laura has .... got back from Europa Park. She got home five minutes ago.
   4 Katia hasn't been to Europa Park .... a long time.
   5 Lorna and Karen have .... been to Europa Park. They are hoping to go there soon.
   6 Adam and Ben haven't been to Europa Park .... 2011.

Word-building

5 Complete the table with the noun and verb form of the adjectives.

Adjective	Noun	Verb
exciting / excited		
worrying / worried		
enjoyable		
relaxing / relaxed		
organised		
challenging		
disappointing / disappointed		
entertaining		

6 Complete the sentences with the correct form of the word in brackets. You may need a noun, verb or adjective.

1 I thought the big wheel was a very .... ride. (excite)
2 She has been more .... since her break at the theme park. (relax)
3 Going to a theme park is a great form of .... (entertain)
4 I don't get much .... from scary films. (enjoy)
5 She's a bit .... about going on the scariest rides. (worry)
6 Some people are afraid of heights, so a lot of rides are a big .... for them. (challenge)
7 I was a bit .... because the rides weren't scary enough. (disappoint)
8 The .... at the theme park is very good. (organise)

7 Look at these sentences carefully. Which pairs of sentences have a similar meaning? Which pairs have a different meaning?

1 a There are some very scary rides at Europa Park in Germany.
  b Europa Park has some of the scariest rides in Germany.
2 a Europa Park opened in 1975.
  b Europa Park has been open since 1975.
3 a Europa Park is visited by millions of people every year.
  b Millions of people visit Europa Park every year.
4 a There is a lot of excitement when a new ride opens at Europa Park.
  b People get very excited when a new ride opens at Europa Park.
5 a There has never been a serious accident at Europa Park.
  b No one has ever been in a serious accident at Europa Park.

Exam task

Here are some sentences about a theme park.

For each question, complete the second sentence so that it means the same as the first.

Use no more than three words.

Exam tip

Think about the changes you may need to make. For example, do you need to change the verb from negative to positive or from past simple to present perfect? Do you need to use the verb form instead of a noun?

1 Luke has never been to Europa Park before.
  This is the .... **Luke has been to Europa Park.**
2 The last time Sarah went to Europa Park was in 2011.
  Sarah .... **to Europa Park since 2011.**
3 The most exciting ride for Sarah was the waterfall ride.
  The ride that .... **Sarah the most was the waterfall ride.**
4 Sarah had a very enjoyable time at Europa Park.
  Sarah .... **her time at Europa Park.**
5 Sarah and Luke are still deciding which rides they want to go on.
  Sarah and Luke .... **yet which rides they want to go on.**

Extreme diets
VOCABULARY — Food & drink

A Sara Harvey: marathon runner

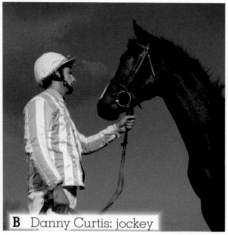

B Danny Curtis: jockey

C Lee Martin: polar scientist

1 Look at the photos. What do you think the people often / never eat before a race or walk? Write their names in the correct place in the table.

Person	Often	Never
1	fruit, yoghurt, fish, salad	fried food, eggs
2	chocolate biscuits, soup, butter, cheese, bread, fried sausages, frozen vegetables, raw fish	salad
3	boiled vegetables, e.g. broccoli, pasta/rice	meat, butter, cheese

2 Match the words from Exercise 1 with the definitions.

1 frozen   **a** uncooked
2 raw   **b** cooked in hot water
3 fried   **c** very cold
4 boiled   **d** cooked in oil

3 Complete the questions with these words. Then ask and answer in pairs.

> fit fitness health healthiest unhealthy unfit

1 Which person do you think has the .... diet?
2 Which of the foods in Exercise 1 are good for your .... ?
3 Which person do you think has to do the most .... training?
4 Which person often eats .... food like biscuits?
5 Which person's diet could make them weak and .... ?
6 Which person has to put on weight to keep .... and strong?

4 Put the food under the correct heading.

> beef cabbage cod corn lettuce peach pineapple
> salmon spinach strawberry tuna turkey

Fruit	Vegetable	Fish	Meat

5 Can you add two words to each group in Exercise 4? Which of these foods do you like / dislike?

6 Match the questions and answers. Then ask and answer the questions with a partner.

1 What's your favourite food?
2 Do you know how to cook?
3 Who's the best cook in your family?
4 What food do you miss most when you're away from home?

a My mum does most of the cooking and she can cook all kinds of food really well. But my dad is very good at barbecues. He does the best steaks. So both my parents can cook very well.

b I can only make fried eggs. I've tried making cakes, but they're not very good.

c When I'm staying at a friend's house or when I'm on holiday, I can't wait to get home and have some of the bread my grandmother makes. It's really good.

d I like all kinds of food, but I definitely couldn't live without chocolate.

5 LISTENING

Part 3

Exam tip

In Listening Part 3 you will often hear two words which could possibly be the answer, but only one will be correct. ✓

1 Complete the sentences with these words and numbers. You can put two words in each space.

> chips   fried egg   53   2007   fruit   55
> ice cream   knee   shoulder   2009

1 Danny started horse racing in ..../........... .
2 Danny misses eating ..../........... .
3 Danny weighs ..../.......... kg at the moment.
4 For breakfast Danny has a ..../.......... and a slice of toast.
5 Danny broke his ..../.......... about two years ago.

2 🔊 21 Listen to Danny and circle the correct word in the sentences in Exercise 1.

3 🔊 22 Now look at the sentences about Lee Martin. Think of possible words to fit in the spaces. Then listen and see if you were correct.

1 Lee often spends .... days camping in the snow.
2 Lee often suffers from sore ....
3 Lee says it's often difficult to cook because of the ....
4 Lee never eats ....
5 The food Lee misses most when he is in Antarctica is ....

Exam task

🔊 23 You will hear a man called Pete Russell giving a talk about an extreme camping trip.
For each question, fill in the missing information in the numbered space.

EXTREME CAMPING TRIP

Training day: (1) ....

Food

Plenty of raw food available

You will learn where to find (2) ....

(3) .... can be quite tasty

No (4) .... on this trip because it's difficult and takes too long

Cooking

You will learn how to use a (5) .... to cook food on

It's important to (6) .... from rivers and streams

4 Would you like to go on an extreme camping trip like the one Pete Russell talks about? Why? / Why not?

5 GRAMMAR

Future forms

G *Page 82*

1 **24** Listen and complete what Pete Russell said. Then answer the questions.

1 'It .... probably rain tomorrow.'
   Is Pete certain about tomorrow's weather?
2 'We .... at 8.30.'
   Is this a decision that Pete has already made?
3 'We .... only what nature can provide.'
   Is this something Pete wants to happen?

2 Match the verb forms with their uses.

1	*will*	**a** to talk about future arrangements
2	*be going to*	**b** to make predictions (often after verbs such as *expect*, *promise*, *hope*, etc.) or to make a decision at the time of speaking
3	the present continuous	**c** to talk about intentions and plans

> **Exam tip**
>
> The present simple can also be used with a future meaning, but only to talk about timetables in the future, e.g. *The plane leaves at 7.30 tomorrow.* ✓

3 Complete the questions with *is*, *are* or *will*. Then ask and answer with a partner.

1 What .... you having for dinner this evening?
2 Do you think you .... ever live in another country?
3 .... you going to have a party to celebrate your birthday?
4 .... your parents let you stay by yourself in the house?
5 What .... you going to do when you get home?
6 .... you travel abroad next holiday?
7 What do you think you .... study when you leave school?
8 What time .... our next class?

4 Choose the correct verb form to complete the dialogues.

1 **A:** I promise *you'll love / you're loving* eating insects.
   B: I hope you're right!
2 **A:** Can you give this book to Ellis?
   B: No problem. *I see / I'm seeing* him tomorrow.
3 **A:** I hope *you're having / you'll have* fun tonight.
   B: Actually, I don't really like parties.
4 **A:** I'm really hungry.
   B: *I'll make / I make* you a sandwich.
5 **A:** What time is your exam tomorrow?
   B: It *will start / starts* at 9.00 a.m.
6 **A:** In tomorrow's lesson *we are learning / we'll learn* how to make soup.
   B: That's good. I love soup.

5 Work in pairs. Complete the table with one idea about yourself for each heading. Then compare information. Find out if there's an activity you're both going to do.

	Prediction	Intention	Arrangement
This evening			
Tomorrow			
This weekend			

> Are you doing anything this evening?

> I don't think so. I think I'll have a lot of homework to do. What about you?

> Tonight I'm going to make a cake for my dad's birthday.

5 READING Health

Part 1

1 Match sentences 1–10 with the correct meaning a–d.

1 Students are required to wear trainers for sports activities.
2 Please throw all food rubbish in the green bin provided.
3 Warning: This water is unsafe to drink.
4 Each student is responsible for making sure the canteen is clean and tidy.
5 Students may bring a healthy snack to school.
6 It is forbidden to eat in the classroom.
7 No students are permitted to touch any cooking equipment.
8 Young people are advised to drink 500 ml of milk per day.
9 It isn't necessary for students to bring a cake to school on their birthday.
10 Students are allowed to use mobile phones during the lunch hour.

a you can
b you can't
c you should/must
d you don't have to (but you can)

2 Where would you see the information in the sentences in Exercise 1?
More than one answer may be possible.

A on a classroom noticeboard
B in an email to students/parents
C in a kitchen
D on a food label

> **Exam tip**
> It's important to understand who the information is for and why they may need it. ✓

3 Choose the correct modal verb in each message, label or notice below.
Then decide who each one is written for.

You *must / could* have the correct change for this machine.

You *should / may* follow the cooking instructions.

1 This notice is for people who want
  a to buy a drink.
  b to know how to change some money.

3 This information is for people who want
  a to know which ingredients to buy.
  b to make something to eat.

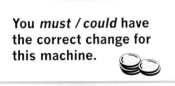

You *may / could* only eat food bought at this café here.

We *could / must* have a picnic, or if it isn't a nice day, what about going to Bunny's for a burger?

2 This notice is for people who want
  a to take food away.
  b to sit down in the café.

4 This email is for
  a a friend.
  b a teacher.

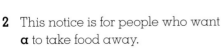 *Page 82*

Exam task

Look at the text in each question.

What does it say?

Mark the correct letter **A**, **B** or **C** on your answer sheet.

Example:

0
> PASSENGERS PLEASE NOTE:
> THERE IS A DELAY OF 10 MINUTES
> ON TRAINS TO EXETER

A Trains to Exeter are all ten minutes late.
B The train journey to Exeter takes ten minutes.
C The next train to Exeter will arrive in ten minutes.

Answer: | 0 | **A** | B | C |

1

To: all students

From: Mrs Long

All students are invited to attend the school's 100th anniversary celebration. Please inform your teacher if you can provide any refreshments for the occasion.

A Students should tell their teacher if they can attend the celebration.
B Mrs Long is informing students that refreshments will be provided at the celebration.
C The school is requesting students bring some food or drink to the celebration.

2

Heat soup in microwave for 3 minutes.

Warning: soup may be very hot.

This label is advising people
A to make sure the soup is hot enough.
B to avoid burning themselves.
C to eat the soup cold if they wish.

3

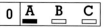

SPECIAL OFFER!

Free delivery service when you order three or more takeaway pizzas!

A Customers get a free pizza if they buy more than three.
B If you buy fewer than three pizzas, you have to pay for delivery.
C This company has just started a delivery service.

4

Study better, play better!

Get the healthy eating habit – choose fresh not fried food

This notice is
A encouraging students to make healthy choices.
B warning students about their bad eating habits.
C forbidding students to eat fried food.

5

Eric

Can you send me your mum's recipe for chocolate cookies? It's Maya's birthday tomorrow and I want to bring some to school. I think she'd love them.

Thanks

Molly

Molly wants Eric
A to ask his mum to make some cookies for Maya.
B to say if he thinks Maya would like some cookies for her birthday.
C to email instructions for his mother's cookies.

5 READING

Part 5

1 Match the phrasal verbs with *go* with the verbs with similar meanings.

1 I can't wait to <u>go back</u> to school.
2 I'm going to <u>go for</u> the steak and chips.
3 Will you <u>go on</u> learning the piano?
4 The price of chocolate has <u>gone up</u> a lot.

a increase
b return
c continue
d choose

Exam task

Read the text below and choose the correct word for each space.
For each question, mark the correct letter **A**, **B**, **C** or **D** on your answer sheet.

Example:

0 A Since **B** From **C** For **D** By

Answer: | 0 | A | B | C | D |

> **Exam tip**
>
> Phrasal verbs are sometimes tested in Reading Part 5. They can be confusing because they look similar, but they have very different meanings – make sure you learn the ones in the study guide. ✓

Should we eat less meat?

(0) .... the 1960s people have eaten more and more meat. One reason for the increase in the popularity of meat is the rise of fast-food restaurants.

Some scientists think the increase in the **(1)** .... of meat that people eat is going to be a **(2)** .... problem in the future because the world's population is **(3)** .... to grow from 7 billion to more than 9 billion. As meat is **(4)** .... more popular in some Asian countries, scientists say that the amount of meat we eat will keep going **(5)** .... What scientists are **(6)** .... of is that it takes a lot of water and energy to grow the crops needed to **(7)** .... farm animals. A lot of land **(8)** .... also needed to grow the food that farm animals eat, which could be used to produce crops for people to eat **(9)** .... However, other scientists say that meat may become so expensive to produce that people won't go **(10)** .... buying it.

	A	**B**	**C**	**D**
1	size	number	amount	total
2	serious	hard	certain	true
3	hoped	thought	known	expected
4	moving	becoming	developing	reaching
5	up	off	on	for
6	afraid	worried	anxious	upset
7	provide	care	give	feed
8	have	is	was	are
9	instead	besides	already	actually
10	up	off	on	for

2 Work in pairs. Discuss these questions.

1 Do you think people will eat less meat in the future?
2 How often do you eat fast food?
3 Why do you think fast food is so popular?
4 What food do you usually go for when you go to a restaurant or café?

5 SPEAKING

> **Exam tip**
>
> Be prepared to answer questions on factual and personal information, using present, past and future forms. ✓

1 🔊 **25** Listen to Astrid answering the examiner's questions. Note down one thing Astrid:

1 likes eating.
2 hates eating.
3 is going to do this weekend.
4 is thinking of doing in the future.

2 Complete the phrases Astrid uses.

1 I'm .... about cooking.
2 I'm always .... for some pasta when I get home from school.
3 I can't .... fish.
4 I'm really .... surfing.
5 There's .... I'll ever leave.

3 Put the words in the examiner's questions in the correct order.

1 favourite / What's / your / restaurant ?
2 going / to / this / are / you / do / weekend / What ?
3 about / something / the / plans / me / your / Tell / for / future .
4 enjoy / after / doing / you / school / do / What ?
5 like / you / cooking / Do ?

4 Match the answers with the questions in Exercise 3.

A Oh, I haven't decided yet. I want to go to university but I don't know what I want to study. I want to travel; to see London and maybe study there.

B I don't like making cakes. It makes too much mess and I hate washing up. But I often help my mum make dinner.

C It depends. If the weather is nice, I might go cycling with my dad. But if it isn't, I'll stay at home and play computer games.

D It's called Milo's. They have the best steak and chips there.

E I like to relax at home. I watch TV, I play the piano and I chat to my friends online.

Exam task

🔊 **26** Listen to the examiner's questions. Take turns to answer with a partner.

> **Exam tip**
>
> Develop your answers with details, don't just give one- or two-word answers. ✓

WRITING

Part 2

W Page 86

1 Look at the example exam task and Suzy's email below. Underline these phrases.

1 phrases for offering
2 phrases for requesting
3 phrases for suggesting

> You are going to organise a barbecue to celebrate your friend Louisa's birthday.
> Write an email to Stan. In your email you should:
> * offer to provide some food
> * ask Stan to bring something
> * suggest Stan comes to your house to help prepare the barbecue.

> Hi Stan
>
> I'm going to organise a barbecue to celebrate Louisa's birthday next Saturday. I'll provide all the meat so don't worry about that. Could you bring something to drink? Why don't you come to my house at 12 on Saturday and we can prepare everything together?
>
> Bye for now
>
> Suzy

2 ⊙ Exam candidates often make mistakes with modal verbs. Choose the correct verbs, then put the phrases under the correct heading below. Can you add any more phrases?

1 I can / may get some milk at the shop, if you like.
2 We can to / could get a takeaway.
3 Could / Should you make me a sandwich?
4 What about / Why don't you come to my house for dinner?
5 We could met / meet at the pizza restaurant.
6 Would you be able to / Should you lend me some money?
7 I will can / I'll help you make a cake.

Suggesting	Offering	Requesting
	I can	

G Page 82

3 Look at a student's answer to the task in Exercise 1. Correct the six grammar mistakes in the email.

> Hi Stan
> I will organised a barbecue for Louisa's birthday. I can to make a cake. Will you can be able to bring some snack? What about come to my house before the party so we could prepare everything together?
> See you soon
> Lulu

Exam task

Exam tip

Always check your writing for mistakes with modal verbs. ✓

You want to help Stefan, who has recently moved to your city, choose a restaurant to celebrate his birthday with his family.

Write an email to Stefan. In your email you should:

* suggest your favourite restaurant
* recommend a particular dish there
* offer to show him where the restaurant is.

Write 35–45 words on your answer sheet.

6 My home
READING House & home

Part 4

1   Look at the photos of two very different homes. Which one would you prefer to live in? Why?

2   Now look at the words and phrases for talking about our homes. Check any words you don't know and write them in your notebook.

> freezing
>
> huge   lively   elderly   sociable
> a garden   a view   cosy   smart   rainy
> cultural events   historical buildings
> traditional   snowy   warm   peaceful   busy
> convenient   comfortable   crowded
> the coast   windy   quiet   kind
>
> in the countryside
> friendly
> plenty of space
> exciting

3   Work in pairs. Student A: do task A, Student B: do task B. Write the words and phrases from Exercise 2 in the correct list, then compare with your partner.

Task A
Which words can you use to talk about:
the weather?   your village, town or city?
rainy   cultural events

Task B
Which words can you use to talk about:
the people you live with?   your house or apartment?
kind   a garden

Did you both use any of the same words in different lists? Check your answers with your teacher.

4   Choose a word from your list and tell your partner the meaning. Don't say the word.

> This word means when the weather is very cold – the temperature is below zero.

> Freezing.

5   Read what a girl called Bea says about where she lives. Complete the text with words from Exercise 2. Then compare your answers with your partner.

I'm from France and I live in a small town near the capital city, Paris. We're in the north of the country, so it can be (1) .... in winter, but the summers are warm. There are trains that run from my town into the centre of Paris, so it's quite (2) .... to get there. We can also get to the (3) .... easily if we want to spend time at the beach, although it's quite a long journey.

The house that I live in with my parents and twin brother is in a narrow street in our town. That means there aren't many cars, so it's quiet and (4) .... Inside our house we have plenty of (5) .... and I have my own room. It's small but it feels really (6) .... and comfortable. My parents are very (7) .... people so we have lots of visitors!

Paris is a (8) .... city with lots to do. My parents love all the cultural events like exhibitions, and I love shopping in the department stores. They're (9) .... – much bigger than the shops in my town! My grandparents live in Paris, in a very (10) .... new apartment. They're quite (11) .... now, both over 80, so my uncle has an apartment downstairs, just below them so that he can help them, although they're still very independent and like doing things for themselves. From their windows you get an amazing (12) .... of the city. I love visiting my grandparents!

6   🔘 27 Listen to Bea and check your answers.

7   Work in pairs. Take turns to talk about where you live. Talk about your town or city, the kind of home you live in and your family. Make a few notes before you begin, and use some words from Exercise 2. What do you like best about your home?

My home town is in …

The rooms in my house are …

The best thing about my town / house is …

Now write three paragraphs about your home. Write about 100 words.

Read the text and questions below.
For each question, mark the correct letter **A**, **B**, **C** or **D** on your answer sheet.

My home is a windmill

by Josh Summers, aged 14

My home's different from where my friends live because I live in a 19th century windmill! My parents saw it one day, and bought it. It was in poor condition, but it was repaired and now it's fantastic!

The windmill was once used to make flour from corn. The corn store used to be downstairs, where our kitchen is now, and horses came there to deliver the corn. The enormous 20-metre sails are still on the front, but they don't turn in the wind like they used to because it's too dangerous, so birds live in them instead. There's always a ladder up the side of the windmill so that dad can paint it and keep it a nice cream colour. He also cleans the windows, although a company comes to do the top ones as the ladder's too short.

Inside it's like a tent with six sides, and it becomes more pointed towards the top, so the rooms get smaller. My room's under the roof and I get a fantastic view – it's like looking out of an aeroplane window. There are some other houses around now, and a new main road, but I can relax and make a noise when I play my guitar up there and no one can hear me! I can hear everything, though, like the birds when it's quiet, which is really calming, or the very loud storms, which I can see coming towards us. And I actually find it easier to concentrate on my school work up there, as my brothers and sisters don't want to climb up all the stairs, so they don't disturb me! I can't imagine living anywhere else!

1 What is Josh trying to do in the text?
   A compare his home with his friends' homes
   B explain why his family chose to live in their current home
   C tell readers about the advantages of living where he does
   D suggest how his home could be improved

2 What does Josh say about the outside of the windmill?
   A Wild creatures have made their homes there.
   B It's covered in dark paint.
   C There's a ladder that goes right to the top.
   D The windows frequently need cleaning.

3 Josh says that his room
   A is a bit like an aeroplane inside.
   B is a good place for practising a musical instrument.
   C is the largest one in the windmill.
   D is better for relaxing in than doing school work.

4 What does Josh say about the different sounds he hears in the windmill?
   A He dislikes the noise of the sails in the wind.
   B He enjoys listening to all the birds.
   C He feels nervous when a loud storm comes along.
   D He's pleased that he's not disturbed by any noise.

5 What would a visitor from the 19th century say if they saw the windmill now?
   A It's great that they've kept the corn store as it was. The horses used to love coming there.
   B The sails are a lot smaller than they used to be. I suppose that's for safety reasons.
   C It's still in the same condition as before. The owners never looked after it then, either.
   D You can still see the windmill from miles away. Of course, there weren't all these buildings around it then, or a busy road going past.

6 GRAMMAR

used to

G *Page 83*

1 Look at what Josh says about the windmill on page 47. Then complete the sentences with the correct form of *used to*.

The corn store **used to** *be downstairs.* (it isn't there any more)

1 .... (you) play computer games when you were younger?
2 I..................... go out in the evenings, but I go out a lot now.
3 My mum .... take me to the park every day when I was small.
4 My older sister .... play with me very much when I was a child.
5 .... (she) have long hair when she was ten?
6 I..................... ride my bike to school every day, but now I go on the bus.

2 Work in pairs. Take turns to ask and answer about things you used to do and didn't use to do when you were younger.

When I was younger, I used to ...
I didn't use to ...
Did you use to ... when you were small?

Verbs followed by infinitive / -ing form

G *Page 83*

3 Look at these sentences from the text on page 47.

My brothers and sisters **don't want to climb** *up all the stairs.*
I can't **imagine living** *anywhere else.*

Complete the table with *infinitive* or *-ing* form.

Verbs followed by	Verbs followed by ....
apologise for, avoid, consist of, imagine, look forward to, suggest	advise, agree, forget, intend, learn, offer, persuade, plan, promise, teach, want

4 ☉ Correct the mistakes in these sentences written by exam candidates.

1 If you agree going with me, you can bring an icy drink.
2 Do you like go to the cinema?
3 I look forward to see you soon.
4 In my country, weddings consist of go to the church and then to a good restaurant.

5 Complete the sentences with the correct form of the verb in brackets.

1 My older sister wants to learn .... (drive) as soon as possible.
2 I can't imagine .... (lose) my mobile. My parents would be very angry!
3 I had to apologise to my mum for .... (break) her favourite vase.
4 My dad offered .... (take) me to my friend's house in the car.
5 Jay suggested .... (go) to the cinema, but I haven't got any money.
6 I didn't really want to go out tonight, but my friend persuaded me .... (go).

do, make, go, have

G *Page 83*

6 Look at what Josh says about his guitar.

I can **make a noise** *when I play my guitar up there.*

☉ Correct the mistakes in these sentences written by exam candidates. Which verb should replace the underlined verb?

1 Why don't we <u>do</u> camping?
2 Anyway, don't <u>make</u> stupid things!
3 If we <u>make</u> a picnic, we'll enjoy it a lot.
4 I hope you will <u>do</u> the right choice.
5 We can <u>make</u> a lot of things like skating.
6 We're good students and we <u>make</u> our homework together.
7 Sometimes we also <u>make</u> a small argument.

6 READING Places & buildings

1 Work in pairs. Think about all the old buildings you can see in your town or city.

Have you been to the main library in your city? A museum? A palace? A castle? What did you do there? What might you expect to see in each of these places?

Exam task

Read the text below and choose the correct word for each space.

For each question, mark the correct letter **A**, **B**, **C** or **D** on your answer sheet.

Example:

0 **A** on   **B** to   **C** by   **D** at

Answer: 0 | **A** ▬ | **B** ▭ | **C** ▭ | **D** ▭ |

Exam tip

Try writing a word in the space before you look at the options. This can help you when you come to make your choices. ✓

The pyramids in Egypt

Last year, my parents wanted to take my brother and me **(0)** .... a special holiday. They **(1)** .... to take us to Egypt, **(2)** .... we could visit the famous pyramids at Giza. I **(3)** .... some homework on them before we arrived, and I found out that in **(4)** .... , they're the only one of the Seven Wonders of the World that still **(5)** .... The oldest and biggest pyramid was built by the pharaoh Khufu and **(6)** .... of over one million blocks of stone!

Lots of visitors come to see the pyramids and I discovered that many years ago people **(7)** .... to climb on them. That's not permitted any more, though, as it **(8)** .... too much damage to the stones. We had our photo taken near the pyramids, and also near the Sphinx, the stone creature a short **(9)** .... from the pyramids. Those photos will always **(10)** .... us of a really special holiday!

1 **A** suggested	**B** persuaded	**C** advised	**D** offered
2 **A** which	**B** what	**C** where	**D** when
3 **A** made	**B** did	**C** read	**D** took
4 **A** fact	**B** case	**C** general	**D** time
5 **A** continues	**B** exists	**C** lasts	**D** lives
6 **A** includes	**B** contains	**C** involves	**D** consists
7 **A** used	**B** allowed	**C** could	**D** ought
8 **A** makes	**B** does	**C** gets	**D** puts
9 **A** length	**B** range	**C** distance	**D** space
10 **A** remember	**B** tell	**C** remind	**D** inform

2 Work in pairs. Discuss these questions.

1 What can you remember about the pyramids from the text?
2 Have you ever visited them?
3 What's the most amazing building you've ever visited?
4 Which place would you most like to visit?

6 WRITING

Part 3

W *Page 88*

1 Match the names with the photos. Would you like to visit any of these places? Why? / Why not?

> the Taj Mahal   the Leaning Tower of Pisa
> the Great Wall of China
> Buckingham Palace   the Eiffel Tower

2 Work in pairs. Look at the places in the box. What would you enjoy about going to each place? What wouldn't you enjoy? Give reasons for your answers. The adjectives in the box below might give you some ideas.

> a city   the coast   a desert   a forest   a jungle
> a lake   mountains   a village

> hot   cold   dry   freezing   snowy
> dangerous   crowded   busy
> quiet   peaceful   boring   exciting

Linking words

> **Exam tip**
>
> When you write in English, think about how to join your ideas together. ✓

3 Read Holly's email about a place she visited. Match the <u>underlined</u> words with the headings below.

> My parents and I have just spent a day in London. It was fantastic!
>
> When we <u>first</u> arrived, we set off to explore, <u>despite</u> the rain! We walked all the way along the river, <u>and</u> spent the morning at Tate Modern, a huge art gallery. We <u>also</u> had a ride on the London Eye <u>because</u> we wanted to see right across the city – <u>and</u> we weren't disappointed! <u>Although</u> it was cloudy, we still saw some wonderful views, <u>so</u> we were very happy. <u>Then in the evening</u> we took a bus tour around different parts of the city, which was great fun, and <u>then</u> we ate in a really nice restaurant. <u>After that</u> we went home. We were tired <u>but</u> very satisfied!

Time links	
Links to explain reason and result	
Links to add a point	
Links to contrast a point	

4 Now look at Jackie's email to a friend about a day at a museum. Complete the email with a linking word from Exercise 3.

> When we arrived at the museum it was still quite early in the morning, (1) .... (result) we decided to go to the café for some breakfast, which was delicious. (2) .... (contrast) the museum had just opened, there were quite a few people in there. Then we set off around the museum. (3) .... (time link) we went to look at the Egyptian section, and (4) .... (time link) we went inside a special room (5) .... (reason) we wanted to see the beautiful old jewellery in there. (6) .... (contrast) it was quite crowded, we managed to see everything (7) .... (add a point) we were even allowed to take pictures, (8) .... (result) that was great! We spent the whole day at the museum. It was quite expensive (9) .... (contrast) we didn't mind (10) .... (reason) we all had a good time!

5 ⊙ Exam candidates sometimes make mistakes with punctuation. Correct the mistakes in these sentences written by exam candidates. In which sentences could you use a linking word?

Exam tip

When you're writing sentences, it's important to think about where one sentence ends and the next one begins. ✓

1 There was a problem, I needed a special card to enter.

There was a problem. I needed a special card to enter.

There was a problem because I needed a special card to enter.

2 It's going to be great, you can bring sandwiches.

....

3 Thanks for your letter, it's good to hear from you.

....

4 We went to swim in the sea, the day was hot and sunny.

....

5 A picnic in the park is a good idea, it's very big.

....

6 My mobile rang, it was Sarah, my best friend.

....

6 Look at the story written by a boy called Alex, about his trip to the beach. Decide where each sentence ends, and put in punctuation. Compare your answer with a partner.

we set off early in the morning the sun was shining and it was hot we had brought a picnic with us to eat on the beach we were quite hungry so we were really looking forward to it finally we arrived at the beach the sea was really blue and it was a beautiful day we got everything out of the car and raced down to the sea my brother and I got changed and went swimming immediately then we ate the picnic it was delicious we spent the whole day on the beach and then came home as the sun went down and it began to get cold it was a great day

🔘 28 Listen to Alex talking about his day at the beach, and check your answers. Can you split the answer into three paragraphs?

Exam task

• This is part of a letter you receive from an English friend.

> For my family and me, the mountains are a special place where we can spend some time together. Have you and your family got a favourite place you all like to go to? When did you last go? What did you do there?

Exam tip

In the exam, you have to choose between a letter and a story. Make a plan – write down a few ideas before you start so that you know you have enough to say about the one you choose. Don't forget to write only about 100 words. ✓

• Now write a letter to your friend.
• Write your **letter** on your answer sheet.

6 LISTENING

Exam task

29 There are seven questions in this part.
For each question, choose the correct answer **A**, **B** or **C**.

> **Exam tip**
>
> Before each recording starts, look carefully at the question and the pictures to make sure you understand exactly what you are listening for.

Example: What do the students agree needs replacing in their school?

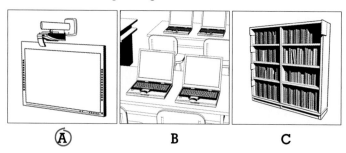

Ⓐ   B   C

1 What does the girl like about her town?

A   B   C

2 What would the girl like to buy?

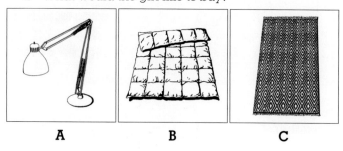

A   B   C

3 What will the weather be like at the weekend?

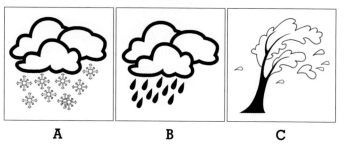

A   B   C

4 What did the boy dislike about the hotel room he stayed in?

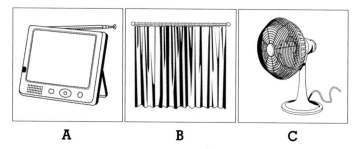

A   B   C

5 Who came to talk to the girl's class at school?

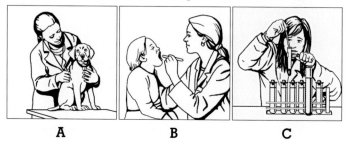

A   B   C

6 Which drink did they have during their school trip?

A   B   C

7 Which birthday present will the girl buy for her sister?

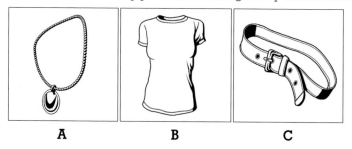

A   B   C

6 SPEAKING

Part 2

1 Put the phrases under the correct heading.

> What do you think?   I think ... would be more useful.
> How / What about taking ...?   I'd prefer to take ... rather than ...
> I'd rather take ...   That's a good idea, isn't it?

giving opinions	making suggestions	asking for opinions

2 🔊 30 Listen to Helen and Tom talking about a trip to the city. Complete their conversation with phrases from Exercise 1.

Helen: Are you all ready for our trip to the museum, Tom?

Tom: Yes, I've got everything. I've put a guidebook in my bag.

Helen: That's (1) .... ? And (2) .... an umbrella?

Tom: I think a coat (3) .... It's going to be cold and windy!

Helen: OK, well, (4) .... an umbrella, I think, (5) .... a coat. I might put one in my bag.

Tom: Fine.

Exam task

🔊 31 Listen to the examiner and do the task.

> **Exam tip**
>
> There is no 'right' answer to this part of the exam. The important thing is the language you use to discuss the options. ✓

VOCABULARY · The natural world

1 Label the pictures with these words.

> bat   camel   elephant   gorilla   parrot   penguin   shark   snake   spider   whale

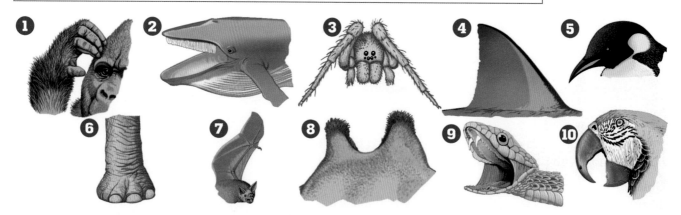

2 Answer the questions about the animals in Exercise 1.

Which animals ...

1 have fur?
2 have wings?
3 are vegetarian?

4 hunt other animals?
5 are deaf?
6 have a good sense of smell?

3 Complete the statements with one of these words.

> wildlife   cruel   rare   protect

1 Many people think it's .... to keep wild animals in cages.
2 People aren't doing enough to .... animals like tigers and elephants.
3 Zoos are a safe environment for animals that are becoming .... in the wild.
4 The best place to see .... is in Kenya or South Africa.

4 Read the notices and answer the questions.

1 Which of the notices A–E do you **not** see at the zoo?
2 Which of the notices is:
   a telling you not to do something?
   b inviting you to do something?
   c making a request?
   d warning you about a danger?
   e telling you when you can do something?

A It is forbidden to feed the animals.

C Sorry, the giraffe house is closed for cleaning. Only staff may enter.

E **Never** leave food in your tent – bears may try to take it.

B Please use the recycling bins provided.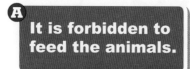

D Talk starts at 3.30. **Lions in Danger.** All ages welcome.

5 When was the last time you visited a zoo or safari park? What did / didn't you like about it?

7 LISTENING

1 🔘 32 You will hear an interview with a man called Martin, who works in a zoo. Look at question 1 from the exam task. Listen to the first part of the recording and answer the questions below.

1 What are the most popular animals at the zoo?
   A the penguins
   B the lions
   C the monkeys

1 Are all the animals in question 1 mentioned?
2 Who says the word *popular*, Martin or the interviewer?
3 What information do you hear which shows the animals are popular?

2 Before you listen to the whole interview, underline the key words in questions 2–6 and the options.

Exam task

Exam tip

The words you hear may not be exactly the same as the words in the options, so listen for words which have a similar meaning. ✓

🔘 33 For each question, choose the correct answer **A**, **B** or **C**.

2 How has the zoo changed in the last 25 years?
   A There is a wider range of animals.
   B The animals have more space.
   C More of the animals have babies.
3 What's the most difficult part of his job?
   A being in dangerous situations
   B getting up early
   C spending so much time cleaning
4 Each day, to stop the animals from getting bored, the zookeepers change
   A the animals' diet.
   B the time they feed the animals.
   C where they put the animals' food.
5 Martin mainly works with gorillas because
   A they need an experienced person to look after them.
   B they like to see the same people every day.
   C they are his favourite animals.
6 Martin was surprised that gorillas are so
   A friendly.
   B peaceful.
   C generous.

3 Look at these adjectives from the exam task. Think of other ways to say the same thing.

1 difficult   *something that is hard to do*
2 dangerous
3 bored
4 experienced
5 favourite
6 friendly
7 peaceful
8 generous

7 GRAMMAR

Past perfect

G *Page 84*

1 Look at the examples of the past perfect. Choose the correct word to complete the statements below.

*The zoo **had already moved** the bigger animals to give them more space when Martin started working there 25 years ago.*
*Martin **hadn't realised** the gorillas were so gentle until he started working with them.*

1 The zoo moved the bigger animals *before / after* Martin started working there.
2 Martin realised that gorillas were gentle *before / after* he started working with them.

The zoo moved the bigger animals.	Martin started working there.

Martin started working with gorillas.	He realised they were gentle.

2 Complete the rule.

The past perfect is formed with the past simple form of the verb .... and the ....

3 🔘 **34** Listen to the news report. Are the sentences true (T) or false (F)?

1 The zookeeper found the tiger.
2 The tiger escaped out of the zoo into the town.
3 No one was hurt.
4 The tiger escaped after breakfast.

4 Listen again and choose the correct option to complete the sentences.

1 A visitor *had / hadn't* phoned the police to say the tiger was missing.
2 The tiger *had / hadn't* escaped before.
3 The zookeeper *had / hadn't* forgotten to lock the cage door.
4 The zookeeper said the tiger *had / hadn't* been hungry.

5 Complete the sentences with the past simple or past perfect form of the verbs in brackets.

1 The zookeeper .... (discover) the tiger .... (escape) at lunch time.
2 We .... (can not) go home until my little brother .... (see) every animal at the zoo.
3 It .... (be) the first time the baby tiger .... (appear) at the zoo.
4 Before I .... (come) to this school I .... (not study) English.
5 I .... (never see) a snake in the wild until I .... (visit) Australia.
6 We .... (go) to my grandparents' house last month, but before that I .... (not be) there for nearly a year.

6 Look at the pictures. What had Super Sam done by the age of 5, 10 and 12?

By the age of 5 Super Sam had learned to drive a car.

5 learn / drive

10 sail / round world

12 leave / university

7 Work in pairs. Discuss these questions.

1 What do you think happened to the zookeeper and the tiger in the story?
2 Have any of your pets ever escaped? What happened?
3 What had / hadn't you done by the age of 5/10/12?

7 READING

Part 5

1 Cross out the verb which <u>cannot</u> go with the noun in each sentence.

1 It's difficult to know how to *avoid / solve / escape* the problem.
2 Some animals *carry / cause / give* a lot of diseases.
3 We need to *find / get / provide* a solution to the problem.
4 A lot of animals are good at *losing / escaping / avoiding* danger.

Exam tip

Collocation (words which often go together) and phrasal verbs are often tested in Reading Part 5, so make sure you keep a record of these and learn them.

2 Which of these phrasal verbs can you use to complete the sentences? Which verb(s) mean a) *to continue* b) *to give*?

| carry on   go on   keep on   pass on |

1 The lion was getting closer and closer but John .... reading his book.
2 She .... some good advice to me about what to do if you see a bear in the forest.

Exam task

Read the text below and choose the correct word for each space.
For each question, mark the correct letter **A**, **B**, **C** or **D** on your answer sheet.
Example:
0 A remove   **B** avoid   **C** stay   **D** keep

Answer: | 0 | A ⎵ **B** ▬ C ⎵ D ⎵ |

The world's most dangerous animal

The world's most dangerous animal isn't a shark or a spider. It isn't a lion or a bear. These animals are, of course, a danger to humans but people can usually **(0)** .... getting too close to them **(1)** .... they are sensible.

The world's most dangerous animal may actually **(2)** .... a surprise. It is, in fact, a **(3)** .... insect, the mosquito. This insect is dangerous because it **(4)** .... diseases like malaria which **(5)** .... millions of people very sick each year.

The male mosquito isn't dangerous. It's the female mosquito that feeds on the blood of animals or humans. **(6)** .... she feeds on an animal which has a disease. **(7)** .... she next attacks a human she can **(8)** .... on the disease.

People have tried to **(9)** .... the problem in many different ways but in some parts of the world mosquitoes are still the **(10)** .... danger to human health.

1	**A** so	**B** although	**C** if	**D** while
2	**A** be	**B** have	**C** find	**D** get
3	**A** short	**B** tiny	**C** thin	**D** narrow
4	**A** carries	**B** takes	**C** lifts	**D** lets
5	**A** put	**B** cause	**C** make	**D** give
6	**A** Just	**B** Always	**C** Even	**D** Sometimes
7	**A** Then	**B** After	**C** When	**D** Later
8	**A** stay	**B** pass	**C** carry	**D** keep
9	**A** improve	**B** help	**C** develop	**D** solve
10	**A** highest	**B** largest	**C** greatest	**D** strongest

3 Work in pairs. Make a list of five animals found in the wild in your country. Which three are the most dangerous?

7 READING — Environment

Part 2

1 How big a problem is litter in your school / town? How do you think people can solve this problem?

2 Complete the statements with these words. Then say which ones you agree with.

| climate change   litter   oil   pollution |

1 I'm worried about .... on the streets. It's a huge problem in this city. People just throw rubbish out of their car window.

3 I'm worried about what will happen when we run out of .... I don't think anyone has found a solution to this problem yet.

2 I'm worried about .... I think sea levels will rise and there will be lots of big floods.

4 I'm worried about .... in the local river. There are hardly any fish in it now.

3 Which of the things in Exercise 2 are you most worried about?

Exam task

The teenagers below all want to do something to help the environment.
On the opposite page there are descriptions of eight charities which help the environment.
Decide which charity would be the most suitable for the following teenagers.
For questions 1–5, mark the correct letter (**A–H**) on your answer sheet.

Exam tip

Underline the *two* or *three* things that are important for each person. Make sure the option you choose matches *everything* they require. ✓

1 Ali has just moved from the city to the country. He is interested in finding out about how to help the wild animals that live in his area.

2 Ramon is worried about the amount of pollution in his area and thinks local wildlife is suffering. He wants to do something about it.

3 Harper has some time at weekends and wants to meet other young people interested in the environment. She wants to organise social events that benefit her local area.

4 Shayna would love to help a charity that works with animals. She has never had a pet, so she would need some help in learning how to look after animals.

5 Saffia lives in a small apartment a long way from the nearest park and wants to spend more time outside when the weather is nice. Her interests include cooking.

Charities working to help the environment

A **Animal Home**

We provide a home for cats and dogs whose owners don't want them any more. We need young people to help us with jobs like cleaning out the cages and preparing food. Have fun and find out about caring for other creatures.

B **Blackrock Zoo Supporters Club**

Join our club and get involved in projects to make the zoo a better place for the animals. For example, this month you could help to build a new tree house for the monkeys to climb on. We also need helpers to give out information to visitors at weekends and to make them feel welcome.

C **Friends of City Park**

At the moment we're building a wildlife area to teach kids about nature. It's hard work but you'll make lots of new friends. We often have barbecues and camping trips at weekends. We need help from teenagers with lots of energy and ideas for other projects to help protect animals in our area.

D **Wildlife Watch**

At our monthly meetings you can learn more about the birds, insects and bats and other creatures in the fields and woods, and also in your garden. You'll find out all sorts of interesting information which will help you provide a better environment for local wildlife.

E **Community Garden Club**

We introduce a taste of the countryside into city life. We can teach you all you need to know about growing vegetables and we even share recipes too. There's no better way to spend a warm summer's afternoon in the school holidays or at weekends.

F **Zero Waste Club**

Start a recycling club at your school. Join our online community and share ideas with other young people who are worried about the amount of waste we produce. The aim is to make your school a zero waste zone.

G **Beach Clean-up Club**

We need more young people to help us pick up all the plastic bottles and bags on the beach. Often we have to take birds and fish that are sick or injured to the animal hospital. We also remove oil from the sand and rocks and check to see if the water is clean.

H **Wild Animal Support Group**

We need young people to help us raise money for conservation projects to help animals in danger around the world. We provide information packs with some ideas about what events you can organise and how to get your friends at school involved too.

4 What can you do to help the environment in your area?

7 SPEAKING

Part 3

1 Tick (✔) the things you can see in the photos below.

> desert   ice   jungle   ocean   river   sunset   waterfall

2 Which of these adjectives can you use to describe the things below (1–3)?

> calm   clear   freezing   frozen   humid   mild

1 the weather
2 the sky
3 the sea / a river

3 Complete the sentences with these words.

> like   must   probably   sure

1 I think it .... be winter.
2 It looks .... it's going to rain.
3 I think the people are .... scientists.
4 I'm not ...., but I think this might be in Thailand.

Exam task

Exam tip

It doesn't matter if you're not sure about anything in the photographs. It's good to speculate about them using phrases like the ones in Exercise 3. ✓

Work in pairs. Student A: Describe photo 1. Student B: Describe photo 2. Try to include as many details as you can about:

- the people: what they are doing / what they are wearing / what they look like / how you think they are feeling
- the place: what the weather is like / where you think it is / what time of year/day the photograph was taken

Exam tip

Start by giving a general description of the photo, e.g. *This photo shows some elephants having a bath in a river.* ✓

4 35 Listen to two students describing the photographs.

➡ *Page 126*

7 WRITING

 Page 86

1 Match the direct statements with the correct reported statement.

1	'I'm having a great time.'	a She told me to have a great time.
2	'I had a great time.'	
3	'I will have a great time.'	b She asked if I'd had a great time.
4	'Have you had a great time?'	c She said she'd had a great time.
5	'Have a great time!'	d She said she was having a great time.
6	'I might have a great time.'	e She said she might have a great time.
		f She said she would have a great time.

> **Exam tip**
>
> In Writing Part 1 you often have to write the direct form from a reported statement. Check you know all the changes that you need to make.

Exam task

Here are some sentences about recycling.
For each question, complete the second sentence so that it means the same as the first.
Use no more than three words. Write only the missing words.

> **Exam tip**
>
> Read the sentences carefully and think about what is being tested, e.g. direct/reported speech, past perfect/past simple, comparative forms, etc.

2  **36** Listen and write the questions.

3 Complete the sentences reporting the questions.

1 The examiner asked Luis if .... Madrid.
2 He .... in the city.
3 He .... in the future.

4 Now practise asking and answering the questions with a partner.

G *Page 84*

1 The teacher told us not to put plastic bottles in the green bin.
'Please .... plastic bottles in the green bin,' the teacher said.

2 The teacher said she had found some interesting information about plastic bottles.
'I .... some interesting information about plastic bottles,' the teacher said.

3 People used plastic bottles to build an exhibition centre in Taiwan.
Plastic bottles .... to build an exhibition centre in Taiwan.

4 This was the first building made of plastic bottles in Asia.
No one in Asia .... a building of plastic bottles before.

5 Building with plastic bottles is cheaper than traditional building methods.
Traditional building methods .... than building with plastic bottles.

6 The children found the programme about buildings made out of plastic bottles interesting.
The children .... the programme about buildings made out of plastic bottles.

5 What do you think about this building? What other things can you make with plastic bottles?

8 We're off!
READING   Transport

1 Work in pairs. Discuss these questions.

 1 What's your favourite way of travelling? By car, bus, plane, train or ship? Why?
 2 Look at the photos. Which of these ways of travelling would you like to try?
 Which ones wouldn't you like to try? Why not?

2 Do we use these words and phrases to talk about travelling by car, plane, train or ship?
Put them under the correct heading. Which words could go in more than one group?

airport	boarding card	check in	crowded	departure gate	feel seasick	flight attendant
hand luggage	harbour	land	motorway	pilot	platform	rough	roundabout	seat belt
security	speed limit	station	take off	traffic jam	traffic lights	waves	weigh

car	plane	train	ship

Compare your answers with your partner. Can you add any more words to each list?

3 Now read what three teenagers said about different journeys they have made.
How were they travelling: by plane, ship or car?

Sarah

> We knew when we all got in that we had a long journey ahead. We looked at the map to see which places we'd pass through, so that we could help dad find the way.

> I had a lot of stuff to take with me, but luckily it wasn't too heavy. After we'd taken off, the attendant brought me a drink and I watched a really funny film.

Mark

> I thought the weather would be unpleasant, but I'd taken a sickness tablet, so I was fine. I just sat and watched the big waves outside the window.

James

4 Are these sentences true (T) or false (F)?

 1 Sarah's father knew how to get to where they were going.
 2 Mark had a problem with the luggage he was carrying.
 3 James' journey was much better than he'd expected.

Look at the sentences below about a submarine trip.

Read the text opposite to decide if each sentence is correct or incorrect.

If it is correct, mark **A** on your answer sheet.

If it is not correct, mark **B** on your answer sheet.

Exam tip

Underline the section of the text where you find the answer. ✓

1 Jon and his family chose to go to America so that they could have a submarine trip.
2 The submarine came and picked up passengers from the beach.
3 Passengers had to allow enough time to check in before their submarine trip.
4 Jon felt confident about being inside the submarine when he first climbed on board.
5 Some scuba divers in the water frightened sea creatures away from the submarine.
6 The shark that approached the submarine was less dangerous than it looked.
7 The weather conditions in the area had damaged an old plane that was under the water.
8 At a greater depth, the range of colours Jon could see from the windows became limited.
9 Jon was disappointed with the photos he took from the submarine.
10 Jon intends to repeat his experience if possible during his next holiday.

5 Work in pairs. Discuss these questions.

1 Would you like to have a trip in a submarine? Why? / Why not?
2 What would you expect to see through the windows?

My Submarine Trip

By Jon Wakefield, aged 15

Have you ever been in a submarine? I got the chance to go in one some time ago – and it was the coolest thing ever! It was while I was on holiday with my family on the coast of America. Dad discovered that submarine rides were available and offered to take me – and of course, I jumped at the chance!

A small boat would come along regularly to collect passengers from the beach and take them to a submarine waiting further out in the harbour. On the day we went, our ride was scheduled for 11.30, but everyone had to be at the beach half an hour earlier, so that there was plenty of time to check in and board. Soon the boat left the beach and we set off towards the submarine.

When we arrived, I was the first one to board the submarine. Space inside was tight, and I felt a bit closed in, and even a little seasick, but then I discovered there were big windows, so I was fine. Then the door closed, and we sank down under the waves. Some scuba divers came down with the submarine and fed the fish right outside the windows. The fish would be too frightened to approach if the divers didn't attract them with food! So we got to see lots of unusual creatures, including sea turtles. There was even a shark that came right up to the windows of the submarine. The announcer said it was one of the smaller, harmless species around there, but it looked pretty huge and scary to me!

As we went a bit deeper, we passed an old plane lying on the bottom of the sea. It was a bit disappointing as there wasn't much left of it after some storms off the coast. There were old ships too, though, and they were a real highlight of the tour.

One thing I didn't expect was that as we went deeper, colours really changed because of the way the water changes the sunlight at that depth. Everything looked either green or blue, so those were the colours in my photos, but it didn't matter. I knew I could just change the colours on my computer once I got home again.

Going in a submarine was one of the best things I've ever done. If we go to the coast again for our next holiday, I'll definitely look for another submarine trip!

6 Work in pairs. Describe journeys you have done by plane, car, train or ship. Try to use as many words as you can from Exercise 2.

I once went to ... by plane / train / car / ship
I went with ...
I took ...
The thing I enjoyed most was ...
I didn't enjoy ...

8 GRAMMAR

First & second conditional

G *Page 85*

1 Look at these examples of the first conditional. Then complete the sentences below so they are true for you.

If we go to the coast again, I'll definitely look for another submarine trip!
If it's not sunny at the weekend, I probably won't go to the beach.
I might call you tomorrow if I need help with my homework.

1 If my friends want to go into town after lunch,
 I... .
2 I...
 if it rains tomorrow.
3 If my mum asks me to go shopping with her,
 I... .
4 I..................... if I get some money for my birthday.
5 If I don't get my homework finished tonight,
 I... .
6 If..,
 I'll ask my dad for some money.

2 Look at these examples of the second conditional. Then complete the sentences below. More than one verb may be possible.

*The fish **would** be too frightened to approach **if** the divers **didn't attract** them with food.*
*I **would be** scared **if** I **saw** a shark!*
*If I **had** some money to spend, I'd **buy** that T-shirt.*

1 If he..................... more careful, he wouldn't hurt himself so often when he's skateboarding.
2 I..................... buy that CD even if I had enough money – I can't stand that band!
3 If I..................... a tiger in the garden, I'd run away!
4 It..................... be great if they closed the school because of the snow!
5 Which country would you visit if you.....................
 lots of money?
6 If I..................... my favourite film star walk into my classroom, I'd scream!

3 Complete the sentences with the correct form of the verbs in brackets. Add *will*, *won't*, *would* or *wouldn't* if necessary.

1 If we don't hurry, we.....*will miss*.....(miss) the bus. We're late!
2 I'd be really sad if I..................... (lose) my watch – it was a birthday present.
3 We probably..................... (not go) shopping tomorrow if it snows – it'll be too cold.
4 If we..................... (wake) up earlier in the mornings, we wouldn't always be in such a hurry.
5 I..................... (not be) very happy if my sister borrowed my clothes without asking.
6 My mum..................... (drive) us into town if you don't want to walk.
7 I..................... (not watch) that film late at night if I were you – it's really scary!
8 If you come to my house, I..................... (help) you make a cake for your mum's birthday.

4 ☉ Correct the mistakes in these sentences written by exam candidates. You may be able to correct the sentence in more than one way.

1 I will be very happy if you came to my house.

2 I think your family would be sad and worried if you don't go.

3 If I were you, I will go to the large school in the centre of town.

4 It would be better if you go to his house.

5 If you will help me, it will be easier.

6 If you come, I would bring something to drink.

5 Work in pairs. Discuss these questions.

What will you do next weekend if:
• your best friend isn't free to come out with you?
• you don't have any money to spend?
How would your life be different if:
• you didn't have a computer?
• you didn't have a mobile phone?

8 READING Travel & holidays

Read the text below and choose the correct word for each space.
For each question, mark the correct letter **A**, **B**, **C** or **D** on your answer sheet.

Example:

0 A had **B** been **C** gone **D** done

Answer: | 0 | **A** | B | C | D |

Exam tip

Read the whole text at the end to check the options you have chosen make sense. ✓

Holidays in space

You've probably **(0)** .... lots of holidays by the beach. So how about trying something **(1)** ....
different – like going into space? Scientists **(2)** .... that if everything goes well, tourists **(3)** ....
soon be able to travel into space on specially designed planes. They could travel as **(4)** .... as 70
miles above the Earth, and enjoy great views in **(5)** .... direction. This would be similar to **(6)** ....
astronauts on board the International Space Station can see now.

The special planes are expected to **(7)** .... off from a 3,000-metre runway. During the flight,
passengers could **(8)** .... up to 15 minutes in space. They'd also have the **(9)** .... to experience how
it feels to float around weightless!

However, tickets are likely to be **(10)** .... expensive – so maybe it's a much better idea to go to the
beach after all!

1	**A** certainly	**B** properly	**C** completely	**D** surely
2	**A** want	**B** wish	**C** need	**D** hope
3	**A** can	**B** will	**C** must	**D** would
4	**A** far	**B** long	**C** distant	**D** fast
5	**A** every	**B** some	**C** all	**D** several
6	**A** who	**B** which	**C** whose	**D** what
7	**A** put	**B** go	**C** take	**D** get
8	**A** spend	**B** use	**C** pass	**D** keep
9	**A** occasion	**B** chance	**C** advantage	**D** luck
10	**A** absolutely	**B** totally	**C** actually	**D** extremely

1 Work in pairs. Discuss these questions.

1 Would you go into space on one of the special planes if you got a ticket?
Why? / Why not? Give reasons for your answer.

2 What would you see from the windows if you were a passenger?

8 LISTENING

Part 4

1 Work in pairs. What are your favourite places to go for a holiday? Look at the photos below. Would you enjoy a holiday in these places? Why? / Why not?

2 🔊 37 Listen to Jake and his friend Marta talking about different types of holiday. What are their opinions of each one? Are they positive (☺) or negative (☹)? Tick (✔) the correct box.

	Jake		Marta	
	☺	☹	☺	☹
the coast				
the mountains				
the city centre				
an adventure park				
a sports camp				

3 Work in pairs. What did Marta and Jake say about each place?

Exam task

🔊 38 Look at the six sentences for this part.
You will hear a conversation between a girl, Joanna, and her brother, Mark, about a horse-riding holiday that they've just been on.
Decide if each sentence is correct or incorrect.
If it is correct, put a tick (✔) in the box under **A** for **YES**. If it is not correct, put a tick (✔) in the box under **B** for **NO**.

> **Exam tip**
>
> For questions 1 and 3 you need to listen to both speakers to get the answers.

		YES	NO
1	Joanna and Mark were surprised their parents let them go away independently.	A	B
2	Joanna was very satisfied with where they stayed during the holiday.	A	B
3	Joanna and Mark were more experienced riders than the other teenagers there.	A	B
4	Mark was worried that he might be injured while he was riding.	A	B
5	Joanna was nervous about riding the first horse she was given.	A	B
6	Mark is looking forward to displaying his photos of their holiday.	A	B

8 SPEAKING

Part 4

1 Work in pairs. Take turns to describe these photos from a Part 3 task. *Page 127*

Which of the activities would *you* try on holiday if you had the opportunity? Give reasons for your answers.

2 🔊 39 Listen to Greg and Tina talking about their holidays. Complete the sentences with what they prefer.

1 I prefer .... to ....
2 I like .... more than ....
3 I don't really enjoy .... as much as ....
4 .... is much better than ....

3 Now listen again. What do they say about why they prefer different things?

> **Exam tip**
> If you don't understand what to do in a task, ask the interlocutor to repeat the instructions. ✓

Exam task

Talk with a partner about whether you prefer a holiday in your own country or a holiday abroad, and the things you like doing while you're on holiday. Use the information below to help you.

Locations	
city centre	forest
mountains	lake
desert	hotel
beach	campsite

Activities	
doing watersports	doing extreme sports
reading	shopping
sunbathing	cycling
sightseeing	walking
sleeping	watching live music

8 WRITING

Part 2

1 Work in pairs. Take turns to describe the photo. Talk about:

the location / the weather conditions / the season / who's in the photo / what's happening

2 The photo was taken by a boy called Neil during his holiday. Now Neil's teacher has asked him to write an email to a friend called Sarah about the photo.

Read Neil's email. He's made some mistakes in it. Find five spelling mistakes, five punctuation mistakes and five grammar mistakes. Compare your answers with a partner.

Hi sarah,

youll never guess what happen during my holyday! I was walked along a road in croatia where there was a lots of water. Sudenly I saw a boy waterskiing along the road it was amazing! Come to my house tommorow so that I can to tell about my trip – and show you my foto!

See you son,

Neil

---

3 In Writing Part 2, you have to write a short email or note, with three points in it. What are the three points that Neil's teacher asked him to include in his email? Work in pairs and write down the three points.

1 ....

2 ....

3 ....

4 <u>Underline</u> the past simple in each sentence. Circle the past continuous. Then complete sentences 1 and 2 below.

I was walking along the road when I saw a man.
My phone rang while I was cycling to football practice.

1 In the examples, the .... is used to talk about the long action – the one that began first.
2 The .... is used to talk about the short action – the one that began second.

5 Complete the sentences with the past simple or past continuous form of the verbs in brackets.

1 I was cycling to school when I .... (see) my cat in a tree.
2 I .... (walk) through the zoo when I saw a crocodile coming towards me!
3 I .... (eat) an ice cream while I was watching TV.
4 I lost my money while I .... (sit) on the bus.
5 I was talking on my mobile when my friend .... (arrive).
6 The students .... (all / talk) when the teacher .... (walk) in.
7 What .... (you / do) when I rang you at eight last night?
8 When I saw my friend in town, he .... (buy) a new T-shirt in a shop.

6 In his email in Exercise 2, Neil wrote *I saw a boy waterskiing*. Complete the sentences in the same way.

1 When I went into the classroom, I heard .... I saw ....
2 When I walked into the café, I saw .... I heard ....

7 Work in pairs. Discuss these questions.

1 Have you ever seen anything strange or amazing on holiday?
2 Have you got a photo that you're very proud of or that you like for a special reason? Describe it to your partner.
3 How often do you take photos?
4 What do you usually take photos of?
5 Why is it important to take photos, especially on holiday?
6 Have you got any photos of when you were very small? Describe them to your partner.

Exam task

You want to send your English friend, Marcus, a photo of yourself on a recent holiday. Write an email to Marcus about the photo. In your email, you should:
- explain where you were when the photo was taken
- tell Marcus why you like the photo
- ask Marcus to send you some of his holiday photos.

Write **35–45 words** on your answer sheet.

Exam tip

Try to learn as many phrases as possible from sample answers and use them in your writing, e.g. *You'll never guess what happened …*

1 Choose the correct form of the verbs.

1 Jack *sits / is sitting* in the living room at the moment, doing his homework.
2 Paul *is getting up / gets up* at 7.00 a.m. on school mornings.
3 *We come / We're coming* from Spain, but *we live / we're living* in Canada for a year – my father *works / is working* here at the moment.
4 Sarah *says / is saying* her dad *cooks / is cooking* the family dinner every Sunday.
5 Peter *really wants / is really wanting* to see the latest sci-fi film at the cinema.
6 Holly's sister *studies / is studying* art at university, but *she's working / she works* in a supermarket this summer.
7 *I don't enjoy / I'm not enjoying* this book very much – it's quite boring.
8 *Do you like / Are you liking* chocolate ice cream?

2 Complete the sentences with the correct preposition.

1 Billy is quite worried .... having to do a test tomorrow.
2 Monika is interested .... learning to drive as soon as she's old enough.
3 No one in the class is looking forward .... doing their homework – it's going to be hard.
4 My grandmother is always afraid .... losing her glasses – she can't see without them.
5 Stella doesn't think she's very good .... speaking English – but she always gets top marks!
6 Michael has always been very fond .... cycling.

3 Complete the sentences with these words.

because   so   and   but   although   or

1 We could either stay at home .... we could go into town.
2 Jack needed to get his hair cut .... he went to the barber's.
3 Simon went to play on his computer .... there was nothing to watch on TV.
4 .... Martin wasn't very hungry, he made himself a sandwich.
5 I've got to do my English homework .... watch a short film for history homework.
6 Football practice was cancelled .... it was too cold to be outside.
7 Gemma wants to go to the cinema .... she hasn't got any money.
8 My project's due tomorrow, ... I'd better finish it tonight.

4 Write the correct word for each description.

1 You need these instructions in a cookery lesson to tell you how to make a dish. r..........
2 In this class, you have to do some acting. d..........
3 Swimming and diving are examples of these. w..........
4 In this sport, you hit a ball over a net with your hands. v..........
5 You can eat your school lunch here. c..........
6 You may have to wear this at school every day. u..........
7 You can exercise indoors in here. g..........
8 These are all the buildings and equipment you have at your school. f..........

/30

1 Complete the sentences with the past simple form of the verb in brackets.

1 Paul .... (not arrive) until after midnight.
2 The coach was angry because Tim and Jan .... (be) late for the training session.
3 Who .... (win) the match?
4 Where .... (Suzy / find) Jack's football?
5 Tyler first .... (become) world champion in 2009.
6 I .... (pay) £50 for my ticket for the match against Holland.
7 I .... (feel) terrible because we lost the match.
8 We .... (not have) tickets so we had to watch the game on TV.

2 Choose the correct form of the verbs.

1 Who *were you talking* / *did you talk* to when I saw you at the cinema last night?
2 Luke had to stop playing football because he *was always having* / *always had* problems with his knee.
3 What time *did you have* / *were you having* breakfast this morning?
4 The match *wasn't starting* / *didn't start* until 3.30 p.m. because of the rain.
5 *Was your dad going* / *Did your dad go* to the station when I saw him drive past this morning?
6 Matthew *ran* / *was running* in the park when he was hit by a cyclist, but he wasn't hurt.
7 What *did Emily say* / *was Emily saying* when you told her the news?
8 The boys were swimming near some rocks when they thought they *were seeing* / *saw* a shark.

3 Choose the correct verb to complete the sentences.

1 He's the best footballer on the team because he never *joins* / *gives* in, even when his team is losing.
2 Please can you *hand* / *get* in your essays at the end of the lesson?
3 Do you *join* / *believe* in ghosts?
4 Why don't you want to *get* / *join* in the game? It's fun.
5 I don't want to go out. Let's *stay* / *get* in and watch a DVD.
6 If you ask them again nicely, your parents may *give* / *join* in and let you have a party.
7 How did you *get* / *stay* in if you didn't have a key?
8 People who *stay* / *join* in and play computer games by themselves all day are wasting their time.

4 Choose the correct word, A, B or C, to complete the sentences.

1 Mark doesn't have any .... He doesn't care if he wins or loses.

A ambition **B** talent **C** luck

2 It's important to .... your disappointment when you lose a match.

A fail **B** hide **C** lose

3 Very few people are lucky enough to .... all their dreams.

A succeed **B** win **C** achieve

4 We ..... the other team by six goals to one!

A beat **B** won **C** scored

5 Sally was very upset when she .... the race against her sister.

A defeated **B** lost **C** failed

6 The last time we .... the championship was in 2001.

A beat **B** won **C** scored

7 I don't mind being .... if I feel the other team deserves to win.

A defeated **B** lost **C** failed

8 Some footballers are rude and don't show the other team any ....

A respect **B** attitude **C** disappointment

/32

3 REVISION

1 Complete the sentences with the correct form of the adjectives in brackets. You will need to add other words.

1 The exhibition about film costumes was much .... (interesting) than everyone expected.
2 The range of sizes in a small shop isn't always .... (big) as in a department store.
3 Markets often have .... (good) prices than shops for some goods.
4 It's .... (difficult) to get into town by car than by bus on Saturdays.
5 The bookshop in town doesn't have much choice, but the local bookshop is even .... (bad) the shop in town.
6 Clothes created by designers are far .... (expensive) than most people can afford.
7 Making your own clothes can be one of .... (cheap) ways of wearing original designs.
8 It's essential to wear .... (comfortable) trainers you can find if you want to go running.

2 Choose the correct word to complete the sentences.

1 We went shopping at the new supermarket, *who / which / where* we found exactly what we needed.
2 Sam asked an assistant in the shop, *who / which / where* found the right size for her.
3 Mark forgot to ask his mum for some money, *who / which / where* meant he couldn't go out.
4 After we'd been shopping, we went to the park with friends, *who / which / where* we had a snack.
5 They hadn't got any T-shirts in the right colour, *who / which / where* was annoying.
6 Lots of people are using the new bus service, *who / which / where* goes straight to the town centre.
7 Jane went shopping in the big department store, *who / which / where* she found the perfect dress for the party.
8 Jon missed the bus into town, so he asked his brother, *who / which / where* gave him a lift.

3 Choose the correct word to complete the sentences.

1 A *market / department* store can often have several floors and sells almost everything.
2 Teenagers usually try to buy the most *fashionable / expensive* clothes they can afford with their pocket money.
3 Customers are asked to try on clothes in the *changing room / café* in a store.
4 It's important to choose the correct *size / style* when you buy clothes, so that they fit properly.
5 My sister always *designs / draws* her own clothes – they look amazing!
6 If customers don't like what they've bought, they can take it back and ask for a *reduced item / refund*.
7 The *store / cash desk* is the place to go when customers need to pay.
8 If there's a sale in the store, many items will be *reduced / increased*.

4 Complete the sentences with some of these words.

silver	bracelet	trainers	sandals	suit
leather	plain	wool	boots	gloves	gold	silk
sweatshirt	earrings	dress	plastic	jeans

1 Good quality shoes are usually made of ....
2 .... are the best things to wear on your feet when you go running.
3 Mark's father chose a .... tie for his meeting rather than one with spots or stripes.
4 It's good to wear .... to keep your hands warm if you're cycling in winter.
5 Many men have to wear a .... for work so that they look smart.
6 Sarah loves jewellery, so she bought a .... to match the necklace she's got.
7 In the summer, people mostly wear .... on their feet at the beach.
8 In a jeweller's shop, you can buy expensive rings made of .... or ....

/32

4 REVISION

1 Choose the correct form of the verb.

1 *I've never been / I never went* to Paris. I hope to go there soon.
2 *Did Victor go / Has Victor been* to the cinema last Saturday?
3 How long *have you known / did you know* your best friend?
4 When *have you met / did you meet* Sophie for the first time?
5 *We've had / We had* our dog since 2005.
6 This is the first time *they ever ate / they've ever eaten* sushi.
7 *My brother's always wanted / My brother always wanted* to go to the Harry Potter theme park so my mum's taking him there for his birthday next month.
8 Where *did your teacher find / has your teacher found* your glasses?

2 Choose the correct word, A, B or C, to complete the sentences.

1 Toni and Gina have .... been on a ghost train.
 A ever 　　　　 **B** never 　　　　 **C** yet

2 Haven't you finished watching that film ....? It's very long.
 A already 　　　 **B** yet 　　　　　 **C** since

3 I haven't seen my cousin in America .... over five years.
 A since 　　　　 **B** for 　　　　　 **C** just

4 Alice is in her room. She's .... got back from school.
 A since 　　　　 **B** ever 　　　　　 **C** just

5 I haven't seen that new Spanish film .... Is it funny?
 A yet 　　　　　 **B** just 　　　　　 **C** never

6 It's a long time .... I've been to the cinema.
 A for 　　　　　 **B** just 　　　　　 **C** since

7 Have you .... been to Disneyworld?
 A ever 　　　　 **B** yet 　　　　　 **C** since

8 I've .... done my homework. It didn't take long.
 A ever 　　　　 **B** already 　　　　 **C** never

3 Complete the sentences with the correct form of the word.

1 The ride wasn't as excit......... as I expected.
2 I thought the film was a total disappoint..........
3 My mum finds horror films enjoy.......... but my dad hates them.
4 A lot of young people don't feel relax......... watching films with their parents.
5 My teacher says I need to be more organis...........
6 You shouldn't worr.......... so much. Everything will be fine.
7 What kind of films do you think are the most entertain..........?
8 People shouldn't be afraid to try new challeng...........

4 Complete the sentences with the correct preposition.

1 Sarah's jealous .... her best friend's success.
2 Luke isn't afraid .... the headteacher.
3 I was very anxious .... my performance in the play, but in the end it was fine.
4 Matt is very serious .... becoming a musician.
5 The teacher was satisfied .... our exam results.
6 Don't get annoyed .... what Sam says. He doesn't mean it.
7 We're very excited .... our trip to London.
8 Everyone was surprised .... what happened at the end of the film.

/32

5 REVISION

1 Choose the correct word.

1 *Could / Should* you lend me £3? I forgot my bus money.
2 Oh no! The shop's closed. Now we *can't / mustn't* get a takeaway.
3 Rob *doesn't have to / mustn't* eat eggs. They make him sick.
4 Our teacher says we *should / may* spend less time watching TV.
5 Hannah *might / can* decide to come to the party if she's feeling better.
6 You *might / could* get your mum some flowers for her birthday.
7 I *need / will* make you some pasta now if you're hungry.
8 It *can / might* be possible to get tickets for the concert.

2 Choose the correct verb form A, B or C.

1 I promise you .... this restaurant.
   A will love   **B** love   **C** are loving

2 We've already decided which restaurant we .... to for dinner on Saturday.
   A go   **B** will go   **C** are going

3 Grandma caught an earlier train. Mum .... get her now from the station.
   A will go   **B** is going to   **C** goes

4 Eat your breakfast! You .... hungry later.
   A are being   **B** will be   **C** are

3 Complete the sentences with a word from the box.

| beef   cabbage   cod   lettuce   peaches   strawberry   tuna   turkey |

1 My favourite kind of fish is white fish like ....
2 My mum always makes me eat lots of green vegetables like ....
3 .... grow on trees – they're a kind of fruit.
4 You don't usually cook .... – you put it in a salad with tomatoes.
5 A .... is a very large bird. In some countries people eat it at Christmas.
6 .... ice cream is pink but the fruit is red.
7 .... is the meat from a cow. You can eat it hot or cold.
8 .... is a type of fish. It usually comes in a tin and people often eat it in sandwiches.

4 Complete the missing words.

1 F __ __ __ __ __ food is kept at a very low temperature.
2 R __ __ food is uncooked.
3 F __ __ __ __ food is cooked in oil.
4 B __ __ __ __ __ vegetables are cooked in very hot water.

5 Complete the phrasal verbs with the correct preposition.

1 I think it's nice to go .... to the same place on holiday each year.
2 Her teacher was surprised when she decided not to go .... with her singing lessons.
3 My sister always goes .... chocolate cake. My favourite is lemon.
4 The price of everything is going .... every day.

/28

6 REVISION

1 Complete the sentences with the correct form of *used to*.

1 I .... have a computer when I was younger, but now I've got one.
2 .... see your friends at the weekends when you were small?
3 My parents say they .... have mobiles in their teens, but they wish they had!
4 Sam's grandfather .... walk to school every day as there was no school bus.
5 .... go shopping in supermarkets with your parents as a child?
6 Ben's dad .... do jobs around the house for his pocket money – so now Ben has to do the same!

2 Complete the second sentence so that it means the same as the first.

1 'You should take a coat with you, Karl,' said his mum.
Karl's mum advised .... a coat.
2 'I'm sorry I forgot your birthday,' said Tina.
Tina apologised for .... Geeta's birthday.
3 'I'll help you with your homework if you like, Jack,' said his father.
Jack's father offered .... Jack with his homework.
4 I don't know what it would be like to live in the mountains.
I can't imagine .... in the mountains.
5 'I'll take you to football practice tomorrow,' said Dad.
Harry's dad promised .... to football practice.
6 Jack's mum never travels home from work at 5 p.m. as there's so much traffic then.
Jack's mum always avoids .... home from work at 5 p.m.
7 'Why don't we go swimming tomorrow?' said Tom.
Tom suggested .... swimming.
8 Richard's dad is buying him a car as soon as he's old enough to drive.
Richard's dad intends .... a car as soon as he's old enough to drive.

3 Choose the correct verb to complete the sentences.

1 Sam's parents complained that his computer game *did / had / made* too much noise.
2 Becky's mum *did / had / made* herself a cup of tea when she got home.
3 It's good to *make / do / have* a shower in the morning – it helps you to wake up!
4 David's dad has to *do / go / make* shopping later as there isn't any food left in the fridge.
5 Steven doesn't think he's going to *go / make / do* anything exciting this weekend.
6 Holly's family *did / had / made* a meal in a restaurant for her birthday.

4 Complete the sentences with a weather word.

1 The temperature up in the mountains was below zero – absolutely f......... !
2 It was so w......... that some trees were blown down and were lying on the ground.
3 It's going to be r......... today, so I'm taking my umbrella.
4 Although it was spring, it was w......... enough to take off our coats.
5 On s......... days, some people have problems travelling because of the road conditions.

5 Choose the correct word to complete the sentences.

1 Most teenagers enjoy living somewhere *quiet / lively*, where there are lots of things to do.
2 The people in this street are very *unfriendly / sociable* – they enjoy meeting their neighbours.
3 It's nice to sit in the park sometimes and listen to the birds singing – it's so *peaceful / crowded*.
4 Jack's grandparents are both in their 80s now – they're quite *young / elderly*.
5 The bus stop is just near our house, so the bus is quite a *convenient / difficult* way to get into town.
6 The museum in the town is so *small / huge* that it's impossible to see everything in one day.
7 Jenna's holiday home is *in the mountains / on the coast*, so it's easy to get to the beach.
8 Karen lives in *a house / an apartment* on the fourth floor of a very tall block.

/33

7 REVISION

1 Choose the correct form of the verb.

1 The tiger *had never escaped / never escaped* before.
2 It was the first time I *went / had been* to India.
3 Last year there *were / had been* a lot of floods.
4 Luke *travelled / had travelled* to 20 countries by the time he was 16.
5 The owners of the factory *hadn't done / didn't do* anything to prevent the fire which destroyed all the buildings last week.
6 We *weren't / hadn't been* sure if we would see an elephant on safari.
7 Susan *hadn't found / didn't find* a dress for the party in time.
8 Mum *had already made / already made* dinner by the time I got home.

2 Complete the direct speech with the correct form of the verb in brackets.

1 He said he'd never seen a snake before.
'I .... (never see) a snake before.'
2 My teacher said we would do a project on the environment next week.
'We .... (do) a project on the environment next week.'
3 She asked me if I had a pet.
' .... (you / have got) a pet?'
4 Jack told me he was going on holiday on Friday.
'I .... (go) on holiday on Friday.'
5 She wanted to know where I'd bought my camera.
'Where .... (you / buy) your camera?'
6 The teacher told us not to use our mobile phones in school.
'Please .... (use) your mobile phones in school.'

3 Write the names of the animals.

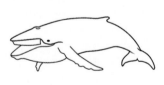

1 w..........

2 s..........

3 p..........

4 c..........

5 s..........

6 p..........

7 b..........

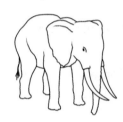

8 e..........

4 Complete the sentences with the correct form of these verbs.

> carry on   pass on   provide
> escape   protect   solve

1 Please can you .... the information about the school trip to your parents.
2 The charity .... a home for dogs that are found living on the streets.
3 The school has increased the amount it recycles but we need to .... the good work.
4 My pet rabbit has .... lots of times, but she always comes back.
5 Everyone needs to do more to .... the environment.
6 I hope scientists will .... the problem of climate change soon.

/28

8 REVISION

1 Choose the correct word to complete the sentences.

1 Sam *won't / doesn't* go out if it's cold tomorrow.
2 *If / Unless* someone helps me, I won't be able to fix my skateboard.
3 If Sophie's dog Ben *sees / will see* a cat, he'll definitely try to catch it!
4 Adam *might / can't* go into town tomorrow if he has enough money.
5 You're late! You *don't / won't* catch the bus if you don't run.
6 William will call *if / unless* he needs anything.
7 I won't buy a new mobile if it *will be / is* too expensive.
8 We *will / won't* know what's in the box if we don't open it.

2 Complete the sentences with the correct form of the verb in brackets or *would / wouldn't*.

1 If Jake .... (not want) to go to the party, he'd tell us.
2 If I .... (be) you, I wouldn't go and see that film – it's scary!
3 Ben .... buy Sarah a present if he couldn't afford it.
4 I wish my sister .... stop making so much noise!
5 What would you say if you .... (win) first prize in a competition?
6 Dan .... be very happy if he lost his favourite T-shirt.
7 Paul's dad would drive us into town if we .... (ask) him.
8 If Jack .... (not stay) up so late at night, he wouldn't get up late in the mornings.

3 Complete the second sentence so that it means the same as the first.

1 It's too hot for us to lie on the beach.
   If it .... so hot, we could lie on the beach.
2 My little brother keeps coming into my room when I'm trying to sleep.
   If my little brother .... coming into my room, I could go to sleep.
3 Dan will have to run to catch the train.
   Dan won't catch the train .... he runs.
4 I don't think you should buy that watch – it's awful!
   I .... buy that watch if I were you.
5 Ben isn't very sociable, so he hasn't met many people at his new school.
   If Ben were more sociable, he .... more people.
6 We can only get the magazines we want if we go into town.
   We can't get the magazines we want if we .... into town.

4 Complete the sentences with the missing words.

1 Drivers have to stop when the t......... l......... turn red.
2 It's useful to take some food and drink with you when you're going on a long j.................... .
3 Passengers have to wait on the p.................... for their train to come.
4 The p.................... is the person who flies the plane when you go on holiday.
5 The bus was so c.................... that there wasn't any room for more passengers.
6 Vehicles can drive faster on a m.................... than on other roads.
7 When you arrive at an airport for a flight, you have to c.................... i......... first.
8 Don't forget to collect your l.................... when you get off a plane.
9 Travelling by boat can be unpleasant if there are big w.................... .
10 It's important to be able to read a m.................... if you don't know the way somewhere.

/32

Unit 1

Present simple

Positive	I / You / We / They He / She / It	go. goes.
Negative	I / You / We / They He / She / It	do not / don't go. does not / doesn't go.
Questions	Do I / you / we / they Does he / she / it	go ...?
Short answers	Yes, I / you / we / they do. / No, I / you / we / they don't. Yes, he / she / it does. / No, he / she / it doesn't.	

The present simple is used:

1 for general truths and facts:
   *Water **boils** at 100 degrees celcius.*
   *The Earth **goes** around the Sun.*

2 to describe routine – things that are done regularly. It can be used with adverbs of frequency, e.g. *usually, often, sometimes,* etc.
   *I **get** up at six o'clock every day.*
   *Ellie usually **goes** shopping with her friends on Saturdays.*

3 for situations which are always or generally true at the present time:
   *It **rains** a lot in Sheffield.*
   *She **lives** in Tokyo.*

Present continuous

Positive	I He / She / It We / You / They	am / 'm is / 's are / 're	going.
Negative	I He / She / It We / You / They	am not / 'm not is not / isn't are not / aren't	talking.
Questions	Am Is Are	I he / she / it we / you / they	watching?
Short answers	Yes, I am. / No, I'm not. Yes, he / she / it is. / No, he / she / it isn't. Yes, we / you / they are. / No, we / you / they aren't.		

We can also say:
He / She / It's not
We / You / They're not

The present continuous is used:

1 to describe something that's happening at the moment:
   *John's **sitting** in the living room and **reading** a book.*

2 to describe something that's true now, but is temporary:
   *I'm **living** in London at the moment.* (but I'm not intending to stay)

3 for events or actions happening in the present but not necessarily at that moment:
   *I'm **learning** Spanish at school.*

-ing forms

1 After verbs of liking, such as *like / don't like, enjoy, hate, dislike, don't mind, love,* etc., the *-ing* form of the following verb is used:
   *I don't **like getting** up early in the morning.*
   *I **love staying** at home and **watching** TV when it's cold outside.*

2 *-ing* forms are also used after prepositions:

*I'm good **at making** cakes.*
*I'm interested **in learning** about history.*

Unit 2

Past simple

Positive	I / You / He / She / It / We / They	watched.
Negative	I / You / He / She / It / We / They	didn't see.
Questions	Did I / you / he / she / it / we / they	go?
Short answers	Yes, I / you / he / she / it / we / they did. No, I / you / he / she / it / we / they didn't.	

Spelling

verbs ending in -e, add -d	like – liked, hope – hoped, save – saved
verbs ending in consonant -y, change the -y to -i and add -ed	study – studied, marry – married, cry – cried
verbs ending in consonant + vowel + consonant, we usually double the final consonant	stop – stopped, plan – planned, travel – travelled
many common verbs have irregular past simple forms	be – was/were, have – had, go – went, give – gave, etc.

The past simple is used for describing finished past events and actions.
It is often used with a specific time reference.
We **played** basketball **yesterday**.
We **didn't go** to the beach **at the weekend**.
Did you **see** Tom at the swimming pool **this morning**?

Past continuous

Positive	I / He / She / It We / You / They	was were	going.
Negative	I / He / She / It We / You / They	was not / wasn't were not / weren't	talking.
Questions	Was Were	I / he / she / it we / you / they	studying?
Short answers	Yes, I / he / she / it was. / No, I / he / she / it wasn't. Yes, we / you / they were. / No, we / you / they weren't.		

The past continuous is used:
1. for describing an action happening at a moment in time:
   *What **were** you **doing** at 3.00 p.m. yesterday?*
   *They **were flying** to Paris at 10.00 a.m. this morning.*
2. for describing something that happened over a period of time:
   *We **were having** problems with our computer last month.*
   *She **was taking** extra Spanish lessons before she sat the exam in March.*
3. for describing an interrupted action. For the action that interrupts the other we use the past simple:
   *We **were having** a picnic in the park when the thunderstorm started.*

Order of adjectives

The usual order of adjectives before a noun is as follows:
opinion / size / age / shape / colour / nationality / material / type + object
wonderful / big / old / round / blue / French / wooden / toy box
awful / small / new / square / pink / plastic / girl's handbag

We don't often use more than three adjectives before a noun:
a beautiful big red box
an old square cotton towel

Numbers always go before the other adjectives:
He's got two pretty older sisters.

With two or more adjectives referring to colour, use *and*:
a blue and white T-shirt
a green, white and red flag

Comparatives

Comparative adjectives are used to compare two people or things:
*This bag is **bigger** than that one.*

Spelling

one-syllable adjectives, add -er	*small – smaller*
one-syllable adjectives ending in -e, add -r	*nice – nicer*
one-syllable adjectives ending in vowel + consonant, double the consonant and add -er	*big – bigger*
two-syllable adjectives ending in -y, remove -y, add -ier	*lucky – luckier*
adjectives of two or more syllables, add *more*	*interesting – more interesting*
some adjectives are irregular	*good – better, bad – worse, far – further*

For some adjectives of two syllables we can either add -er or use *most*. These are adjectives ending in -ow, -le, -er and *polite*, *quiet* and *common*:
*Sally is **more polite** than me. = Sally is **politer** than me.*

To compare two or more people, animals or objects we use *than*:
*My grandmother's house is **smaller than** ours.*
*I think this science book is **more interesting than** that one about history.*

Comparatives can also be made with *not as ... as*:
*That book about history is**n't as interesting as** this science book.*

Superlatives

Superlative adjectives are used to compare one person or thing to the rest of its group:
*This is the **biggest** bag in the shop.*

Spelling

one-syllable adjectives, add -est	*small – smallest*
one-syllable adjectives ending in -e, add -st	*nice – nicest*
one-syllable adjectives ending in vowel + consonant, double the consonant and add -est	*big – biggest*
two-syllable adjectives ending in -y, remove -y, add -iest	*lucky – luckiest*
adjectives of two or more syllables, add *most*	*interesting –most interesting*
some adjectives are irregular	*good – best, bad – worst, far – furthest*

For some adjectives of two syllables we can either add -er or use *most*. These are adjectives ending in -ow, -le, -er and *polite*, *quiet* and *common*:
*Tia is **the cleverest** girl in the class. = Tia is the **most clever** girl in the class.*

Using pronouns *who / which / where*

The pronouns *who*, *which* and *where* can be used to add extra information to sentences. *Who* is used to refer to people, *which* for things, and *where* for places:
I've got a friend called Sue. She lives in Lisbon.
*I've got a friend called Sue **who** lives in Lisbon.*
I bought a dress yesterday. It is really pretty.
*I bought a dress yesterday **which** is really pretty.*
There's a great new bookshop in town. You can buy all the latest magazines there.
*There's a great new bookshop in town **where** you can buy all the latest magazines.*

Present perfect

Positive	I / You / We / They	have / 've	made a film.
	He / She / It	has / 's	
Negative	Have	I / you / we / they	been away?
	Has	he / she / it	
Questions	Have	you / we / they	met her?
	Has	he / she / it	
Short answers	Yes, I / you / we / they have. / No, I / you / we / they haven't. Yes, he / she it has. / No, he / she / it hasn't.		

The present perfect is used:

1 for talking about things which started in the past and are still continuing in the present:
   *I **have lived** in this town for eight years.*
   *He **has been** at this school since 2011.*

2 for talking about past experiences which refer to an unstated time in the past:
   *I've only **been** to New York once. (we don't know when)*
   *They**'ve travelled** a lot. (at various times in the past)*

3 for talking about recent past actions:
   ***Have** you **done** your homework?*
   *It**'s stopped** raining.*

4 for talking about past actions which have a result in the present:
   *I**'ve lost** my keys! (I can't get in the house now.)*
   *He**'s broken** his leg. (He can't play football.)*

5 to refer to a period of time which is not yet finished. Notice the difference between the present perfect and the past simple:
   *He**'s worked** hard all morning. (it's still morning)*
   *He **worked** hard all morning. (it's now the afternoon)*

For and *since* are often used with the present perfect. *For* is used to talk about a period of time. *Since* is used to talk about a point in time:
*I've been here **for three weeks**.*
*I've been here **since Tuesday**.*

Never is often used instead of a negative to talk about past experience:
*I **have never visited** China.*

Ever is often used in questions to ask about past experiences:
***Have** you **ever met** a famous person?*
***Has** she **ever ridden** a camel?*

Yet is used with negatives to show that something hasn't happened but is expected to at some point in the future:
*She **hasn't visited** her aunt in Australia yet. (but she will one day)*
*They **haven't arrived yet**. (but they will soon)*

Just is used to emphasise that something has happened recently:
*The film **has just finished**. (only a couple of minutes ago)*

Already is used to show that something has happened before an expected time:
***Have** you **already finished** your homework? (sooner than expected)*
*I**'ve already spent** all my money. (too soon)*

Yet is used with questions and negatives to talk about things which were expected to happen recently:
***Have** you **bought** your mum a birthday present **yet**?*
*They **haven't decided** which film to see **yet**.*

He's worked hard all morning.   He worked hard all morning.

Future forms

Will

will + infinitive (without to)

Will is used:
1 when something is decided at the moment of speaking:
   It's raining. I**'ll stay** at home today.
2 to make future predictions. It's often used after verbs like think, expect, hope:
   I **think** it **will rain** at the weekend.
   I **hope** she **won't be** late.
3 to make offers and promises:
   I**'ll help** you with your homework.
   I**'ll bring** your scarf to school tomorrow.
4 to ask someone to do something:
   Please **will** you **help** me?
5 to refuse to do something:
   No, I **won't do** my homework – I'm watching a film.

Be going to

am / is / are + going to + infinitive

Going to is used:
1 to talk about plans and intentions:
   I**'m going to do** all my homework this evening.
   I**'m going to be** famous one day.
2 to make predictions based on facts and when we are sure of something:
   Look at the clouds. It**'s going to rain**.
   He hasn't studied at all and he's terrible at maths. He**'s going to fail** the exam.
3 when something is about to happen:
   Be careful! The ladder's **going to fall** over.

Present continuous

The present continuous is used for talking about definite future arrangements. It is often used with a time expression:
She**'s getting** married in June.
We**'re meeting** Leo at 6.30.

Present simple

The present simple is only used with a future meaning for talking about timetables:
The film **starts** at 7.30.
The train **leaves** at 4.15.

Modals

1 Must and have to are used to show that it's essential to do something. We often use must when the obligation comes from the person speaking or listening. We often use have to when someone or something else makes the action necessary:
   You **must** wear a helmet when you cycle. (I'm telling you to.)
   She **has to** stay in bed because she's ill. (The doctor told her to.)
2 Mustn't is used to show something is prohibited, not allowed:
   You **mustn't** use your mobile phone in class.
3 May is used to ask for and give permission to do something. It is rather formal:
   You **may** eat your sandwiches here.
   May I sit here?
4 Should is used to say that something is a good idea or to give advice:
   You **should** read the notice very carefully.
   You **shouldn't** drink the water here.

Suggesting, offering, requesting

To make suggestions use:
1 Shall + I / we + infinitive:
   Shall we go to the cinema?
2 Could + infinitive (without to):
   You **could buy** your dad a book.
3 Should + infinitive (without to):
   We **should ask** the teacher to help us.
4 What about + -ing:
   What about making a cake instead of buying one?
5 Why don't + infinitive:
   Why don't you **wear** your red dress?

To make offers use:
1 will + infinitive (without to):
   I**'ll help** you do your homework.
2 Shall I / we … + infinitive (without to):
   Shall I open the window?
3 Can I … + infinitive (without to):
   Can I make you a sandwich?
4 Would you like me / us to … + infinitive:
   Would you like me to cook dinner?

To make requests use:
1 Can + you + infinitive (without to) (informal):
   Can you lend me your dictionary?
2 Will + you + infinitive (without to) (informal):
   Will you speak to the teacher about it?
3 Could + you + infinitive (without to) (formal):
   Could you repeat that, please?
4 Would you be able to …? (formal):
   Would you be able to come to my party on Saturday?

Unit 6

Used to

Positive	I / You / He / She / It / We / They	used to	play
Negative	I / You / He / She / It / We / They	did not / didn't use to	
Questions	Did I / you / he / she / it / we / they	use to play?	
Short answers	Yes, I / you / he / she / it / we / they did. / No, I / you / he / she / it / we / they didn't.		

Used to is used for describing habit or states in the past which are no longer true for the present:
*I **used to ride** my bike every day.* (but now I don't)
*She **used to study** Chinese.* (but now she doesn't)
*I **didn't use to like** football.* (but now I do)
*They **didn't use to eat** sushi.* (but now they do)
***Did** you **use to play** tennis with your brother?*
***Did** he **use to walk** to school?*

We use *used to* for talking about something we often did or something that often happened in the past but that has changed now.

Remember that *used to* is only used to talk about habits or states in the past. For habits or states in the present use the present simple:
They used to go skiing every winter.
They go skiing every winter.

Verbs followed by infinitive / -ing form

If a verb is followed by another verb, the second verb is either in the *-ing* form or the infinitive, with or without *to*.

1 Some verbs can be followed by either form with no difference in meaning, e.g. *begin, continue, like, love, prefer, start*.
   *I **like reading** at breakfast. = **I like to read** at breakfast.*
   *She **continued studying**. = She **continued to study**.*

2 Some verbs are followed only by the *-ing* form, e.g. *admit, consider, detest, enjoy, can't help, finish, suggest*.
   *I've almost **finished doing** my homework.*
   *Jack **suggested going** to the cinema tonight.*

3 Some verbs are followed only by *to* + infinitive, e.g. *agree, ask, expect, happen, hope, intend, promise, persuade, refuse, would like*.
   *I've **persuaded** my cousin **to come** shopping with me tomorrow.*
   *I'**d like to go** home quite soon.*

4 Some verbs are followed by infinitive without *to*, e.g. *let, make*.
   *My parents **don't let** me **stay** out late.*
   *My mum **made** me **do** my homework before I went out.*

5 Some verbs change their meaning depending on whether they are followed by *-ing* or *to*, e.g. *remember, forget, stop, try*.
   *He **remembered to do** his homework.* (He did his homework – he didn't forget.)
   *She **remembered meeting** him years before.* (She had the memory of meeting him.)
   *They **stopped to speak** to their friend.* (They stopped another activity to speak.)
   *We **stopped watching** TV.* (We didn't watch any more TV.)

do, make, go, have

Do and *make* are often confused in set expressions.

1 *Do* is used to talk about work, jobs and activities:
   *You must **do your homework** tonight.*
   *Can you **do the shopping** later?*

2 *Make* is generally used to talk about creating or producing something. It is also used in many expressions, e.g.:
   make your bed, make a choice, make friends, make a mistake, make a phone call, make up your mind.

3 *Go* is often used with gerunds, e.g.:
   go swimming, go camping, go shopping.

Other set expressions:
go to bed, go home, go to school
have a picnic, have an argument
do damage to sth, do well, do badly, do your best, do your hair

Note that in English we often use *have* in an expression where other languages use *do* instead, e.g.: *have breakfast, have lunch, have dinner, have a shower.*

Past perfect

Positive	I / You / He / She / It / We / They	had / 'd	worked.
Negative	I / You / He / She / It / We / They	had not / hadn't	
Questions	Had I / you / he / she / it / we / they	worked?	
Short answers	Yes, I / you / he / she / it / we / they had. / No, I / you / he / she / it / we / they hadn't.		

The past perfect is used to talk about an event which happened before another event in the past:
*When I got up this morning my dad **had** already **left** for work.*

The past perfect is usually used in a sentence with another verb in the past simple and a time phrase, e.g. *before, by the time, until*:
*I **hadn't eaten** raw fish until I visited Japan.*
*By the time we **left** the cinema, it **had stopped** raining.*
*Before I **met** Jack, I **had never met** anyone from Australia.*

Reported speech

Reported speech is used to report what someone says:
Direct speech: *'I'm hungry,' said Tom.*
Reported speech: *Tom said he was hungry.*

Tenses usually change between direct and reported speech:

Direct speech	Reported speech
present simple	past simple
present continuous	past continuous
present perfect	past perfect
past simple	past perfect
past perfect	no change
might / could	no change
must	had to
mustn't	no change
will	would
would	no change

Some words describing time and place also change (if we are reporting something at a later date or in a different place):
*'The match is **tomorrow**,' my teacher said.*
*My teacher told me that the match was **the next day**.*

Direct speech	Reported speech
today	that day
tomorrow	the next day
yesterday	the day before
last week	the previous week
here	there
this	that

Pronouns and possessive adjectives can also change:
*'**I** came to **your** house this morning,' she said.*
*She said that **she** had come to **my** house that morning.*

Say and *tell* in reported speech

We use *say* if we don't mention the person who is being spoken to:
He said (that) he was going to be late.
We always use *tell* with a direct object:
She told me she could speak French.

Reported questions

Reported questions follow the same rules for tense changes as reported statements. But remember that we don't use the question word order or question marks (?):
*'**Where do** you **live**?' the policeman asked.*
*The policeman asked **where I lived**.*
*'**When did** you **lose** your homework?' asked my teacher.*
*My teacher asked me **when I had lost** my homework.*

For *yes / no* questions use *ask if* or *ask whether*:
'Are you hungry?' asked Mum.
*Mum asked me **if I** was hungry.*
'Do you study German at school?' asked John.
*John asked me **whether** I studied German at school.*

Unit 8

First conditional

If + present simple	*will / won't* + infinitive
If we go now, If we don't go now,	we'll be early. we'll be late.

The first conditional is used to talk about things that are likely or possible in the future:
If we **see** John, we**'ll invite** him to the party.
If I get all my homework done now, **I won't have** anything to do tomorrow.

We can also put the *if*-clause second, without using a comma:
She'll be very angry if she sees you here.
We won't go to the park if it starts raining.

Unless + positive verb can also be used instead of *if* + negative verb:
*I won't go into town **if I don't have** any money to spend. = I won't go into town **unless I have** some money to spend.*

Second conditional

If + past simple	*would / wouldn't* + infinitive
If I left now, If he didn't watch the film,	I'd get there on time. he wouldn't be scared.

The second conditional is used to talk about things that are imaginary, impossible or unlikely:
*If he **practised** the piano more, he**'d play** it much better.* (but he doesn't practise (he prefers to play football), so he doesn't play it any better)
*If she **watched** a horror film, she probably **wouldn't like** it!* (so she's unlikely to watch one)
*If I saw a ghost, I'd definitely **run** away!* (but I don't believe in ghosts, so that's impossible!)

We can also put the *if*-clause second, without using a comma:
They'd go on a cruise if they had the money.
You'd be happier if you didn't worry so much.

Could / might can be used instead of *would*:
She might be annoyed if you told her.
If I studied more I could go to university.

Unless + positive verb can also be used instead of *if* + negative verb:
*I wouldn't help her **if I didn't want** to. = I wouldn't help her **unless I wanted** to.*

With *be* we usually use *were* in all forms:
If I were you, I wouldn't do it.
If her mother were rich, she wouldn't work.

If he practised the piano more, he'd play it much better.

WRITING FILE

There are three parts in the Writing component. You must do all three parts. There is a total of 25 marks, which represents 25% of the total of the whole Preliminary for Schools examination.

Writing Part 1

Questions 1–5
Sentence transformations
5 marks

In this part of the test you are given five sentences which are all about one topic or theme. Each of these sentences is followed by an incomplete sentence. You have to complete these sentences so that they have the same meaning as the sentence before. The beginning and end of each sentence is given and you should only write between one and three words to complete each one.
For more information and practice see units 4 and 7.

Writing Part 2

Question 6
Short message
5 marks

In this part of the test you must write a short message of between 35 and 45 words. You are given some information and told who to write to and why. You always have to include three points in the message. The message may be an email, a card or a note.

Planning and timing

It's very important to understand what the situation is, so make sure you read the instructions carefully. Spend a couple of minutes planning your answer. Think about the kind of language you need to use for each point. Spend about five minutes writing your message and remember to leave yourself a couple of minutes at the end to check you have included all the necessary information and that your message is easy to understand.

To get full marks you need to:
- cover all three points
- use appropriate language for advising / inviting / suggesting, etc.
- begin and end your message in an appropriate way
- write the correct number of words
- make your message clear and easy to understand
- make your writing as accurate as possible (but you won't lose marks for small mistakes that don't cause a problem for the reader).

Useful language

Beginning your message to a friend
Dear + name / Hi + name

Ending your message to a friend
See you soon / Love / Bye for now

Advising
I think you should ...
The best thing to do is ...

Apologising
I'm really sorry about the ...
I want to tell you how sorry I am about ...
I'm sorry I ...

Giving an opinion
I think ...
In my opinion ...

Offering
I can ... if you like
If you want, I could ...
Shall I ...?

Inviting
Would you like to ...?

Saying yes to an invitation
I'd love to ...
That would be great.

Saying no to an invitation
I'm sorry I can't ...

Requesting
Could you ...?

Stating a preference
I'd prefer to ...
I'd rather ...

Suggesting
Why don't you ...?
What / How about ...ing?

Sample tasks

Question 6

You need to borrow a bicycle from your friend Sam.
Write an email to Sam. In your email you should:
- ask to borrow his bicycle
- explain why you need it
- promise to give it back soon.

Write **35–45 words** on your answer sheet.

Sample answer

Hi, Sam
Can I borrow your bike tomorrow? I need
it because I have to go to my friend's
house and there isn't a bus which goes
there. I'll need it for four days, no more,
so on Friday I'm going to return it.
Thanks
Danny

Comment

This is a very good answer
All three points are covered.
Appropriate language for asking (*Can I ...?*) and explaining
(*because*) is used.
The email begins and ends appropriately.
The message is clearly communicated and is the right length.
There are no grammar or spelling errors.

Question 6

You want to invite your friend Alex to have a
picnic in the park at the weekend.
Write an email to Alex. In your email you
should:
- say why you want to meet in the park
- suggest an activity you can do
  together
- ask him to bring something.

Write **35–45 words** on your answer sheet.

Sample answer

Hi Alex!

It is going to be a nice week-end.
So, shall we go to a picnic in the
park on Saturday? I think the
park is best place for a picnic
because in the park we can play
volleyball and we can have good
time easyly. And when you will
come can you bring a ball, please?

Love,

Comment

It's a good answer.
The answer covers all three points.
There is a range of structures used.
The message is clearly communicated but is
a bit too long.
There are six errors (four grammar
and two spelling) which do not impede
communication.

Writing Part 3

In this part of the test you have a choice. You can <u>either</u> do an informal letter (question 7) <u>or</u> a story (question 8).

Question 7

Informal letter
15 marks

For the letter you are given part of a letter from a friend, which provides the topic you have to write about. You should write about 100 words.

Planning and timing

If you decide to do the letter, you should spend time thinking about how to organise your ideas before you start writing. Spend a few minutes making some notes. You need to make sure you write about all the points in the friend's letter, and answer any questions in it. You need to organise your ideas, and open and close the letter in a suitable way. You should spend about fifteen minutes writing your letter, and then another two or three minutes reading it through to check that it's easy to understand. Correct any grammar, spelling or punctuation mistakes you have made.

To get full marks you need to:
- make sure you have written about the topic in the friend's letter, and answered any questions in it.
- write the correct number of words. If you write too much, you may make more mistakes, and you may not have enough time at the end to check your answer.
- use a range of structures and vocabulary related to the topic.
- open and close the letter in a suitable way – but don't write too much at the beginning and the end. The main part of your letter must be about the topic.
- make as few mistakes as possible. It must be clear to the reader what you are trying to say.

Useful language

Opening a letter	Closing a letter
Hi, Dan	*Looking forward to hearing from you.*
Dear Dan	*See you soon.*
How are you? I hope you're well.	*Best wishes*
It was nice to hear from you / get your letter.	*All the best*
Thanks for your letter.	*Write back soon.*
	Love

Thanking
> *Thanks for ...ing.*

Suggesting
> *How / What about ...ing?*
> *Why not ...? / Why don't you ...?*
> *You could ...*

Giving advice
> *You should / shouldn't ...*
> *If I were you, I would / wouldn't ...*

Adding a similar point
> *Besides this ...*
> *What's more ...*
> *Another important thing is that ...*
> *Also ...*

Adding a contrasting point
> *However ...*
> *On the other hand ...*
> *... but ...*

Adjectives

amazing	brilliant	awful
wonderful	enjoyable	disappointing
fantastic	incredible	disgusting
beautiful	lively	frightening
excellent	reasonable	dull
lovely	magnificent	unpleasant
stylish	smart	

Sample task

Write an answer to **one** of the questions (**7** or **8**) in this part.
Write your answer in about **100 words** on your answer sheet.
Mark the question number in the box at the top of your answer sheet.

Question 7

- This is part of a letter you receive from a friend.

> I went for a meal in a new restaurant with my family last week. It was fantastic! Have you got a favourite restaurant that you enjoy going to? Write and tell me all about it!

- Now write a letter, answering your friend's question.
- Write your **letter** on your answer sheet.

Sample answer

Dear George,

It was nice to hear from you. What does the new restaurant look like? Maybe we could go together next week. Is it a Chinese restaurant? My favourite restaurant is an Italian one. I love Italian food. I could live happily just eating it. The restaurant is enchanting. It has an amazing view of a lake. The service is excellent also. I really like going there with friends and or even alone. It's lovely I think you would like it as well. How about going there next Saturday? I can make a reservation if you want to go. Write back!

Love,

Maria

Comment

This is a very good answer.
The letter answers the question in the friend's letter, and gives a lot of information.
The letter opens and closes suitably.
The friend would clearly understand the letter, and it is the right length.
A range of structures is used (*What does ... look like? Maybe we could ... I really like going ... How about going ...? if you want*).
There is also a good range of adjectives (*enchanting, amazing, excellent, lovely*).
There are a few errors (*The service is excellent also. It's lovely I think you would like it as well*) – but the message is clear.

Writing Part 3

Question 8

Story
15 marks

For the story you are either given the first sentence of the story to continue or the title. You should write about 100 words.

Planning and timing

It's very important to spend a minute or two deciding whether you should choose the story or the informal letter. You need to think about the topic of the story carefully and decide if you have the ideas and the language to write this story well.

If you decide to do the story, you need to plan how you will organise your ideas. It's worth spending a few minutes making some quick notes. You should think about how to begin and end your story so that it's interesting to read. You also need to think about the tenses you need to use.

You should spend about fifteen minutes writing your story and then another two or three minutes reading it through to check that it's easy to understand and correcting any grammar, spelling or punctuation mistakes.

To get full marks you need to:
- make sure your story links to the title or the first sentence in the task. Don't write pre-prepared stories as these will not fit the task.
- write the correct number of words. (Answers that are too short cannot get full marks.)
- use a range of structures and vocabulary. Don't use language that is very simple and repetitive.
- make your story interesting for the reader by having a good beginning and ending and by using a variety of adjectives and adverbs.
- make your story easy to follow by using linking words and appropriate pronouns.
- make your writing as accurate as possible, but you won't lose marks for small mistakes which don't cause a problem for the reader.

Sample task

Write an answer to one of the questions (**7** or **8**) in this part.
Write your answer in about **100 words** on your answer sheet.
Mark the question number in the box at the top of your answer sheet.

Question 8

- Your English teacher has asked you to write a story.
- Your story must begin with this sentence:
  I was really surprised when I opened the box.
- Write your **story** on your answer sheet.

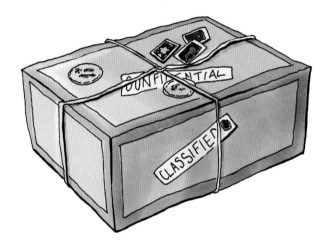

Sample answer

I was really surprised when I opened the box. It was Sunday evening and I was very tired because I had gone out all the day with my friends. I was in my bed reading a book when I heard a noise. It came from the room near mine. I thougth it was the wind and so I continued to read my book. But it started again. I decided to go there and when I opened the door I found a little turtle in the box. It was so beautiful. The next day I told my brother. We decided to take care of the turtle. This was our first secret.

Comment

This is a very good answer.
The story links to the task well, although it would be better if the box was referred to again earlier in the story after the opening sentence. It is interesting and easy to understand. A range of structures is used (past simple, past perfect, past continuous). Linking words are used effectively (*But, when, The next day*). Some descriptive language is used (*beautiful, little*). It isn't too long or too short. The spelling mistake (*thougth*) does not cause a problem for the reader.

IRREGULAR VERBS

verb	past simple	past participle
be	was / were	been
beat	beat	beaten
become	became	become
begin	began	begun
bend	bent	bent
bite	bit	bitten
bleed	bled	bled
blow	blew	blown
break	broke	broken
build	built	built
burn	burnt / burned	burnt / burned
buy	bought	bought
catch	caught	caught
choose	chose	chosen
come	came	come
cost	cost	cost
cut	cut	cut
deal	dealt	dealt
dig	dug	dug
do	did	done
draw	drew	drawn
dream	dreamt / dreamed	dreamt / dreamed
drink	drank	drunk
drive	drove	driven
eat	ate	eaten
fall	fell	fallen
feed	fed	fed
feel	felt	felt
fight	fought	fought
find	found	found
fly	flew	flown
forbid	forbade	forbidden
forget	forgot	forgotten
forgive	forgave	forgiven
freeze	froze	frozen
get	got	got
give	gave	given
go	went	gone
grow	grew	grown
hang	hung	hung
have	had	had
hear	heard	heard
hide	hid	hidden
hit	hit	hit
hold	held	held
hurt	hurt	hurt
keep	kept	kept
kneel	knelt	knelt
know	knew	known
lay	laid	laid
lead	led	led
learn	learnt / learned	learnt / learned
leave	left	left

verb	past simple	past participle
lend	lent	lent
let	let	let
lie	lay	lain
lose	lost	lost
make	made	made
mean	meant	meant
meet	met	met
pay	paid	paid
put	put	put
read	read	read
ride	rode	ridden
ring	rang	rung
rise	rose	risen
run	ran	run
say	said	said
see	saw	seen
sell	sold	sold
send	sent	sent
set	set	set
sew	sewed	sewn
shake	shook	shaken
shine	shone	shone
shoot	shot	shot
show	showed	shown
shut	shut	shut
sing	sang	sung
sink	sank	sunk
sit	sat	sat
sleep	slept	slept
smell	smelt / smelled	smelt / smelled
speak	spoke	spoken
spell	spelt / spelled	spelt / spelled
spend	spent	spent
spill	spilt / spilled	spilt / spilled
spoil	spoilt / spoiled	spoilt / spoiled
stand	stood	stood
steal	stole	stolen
stick	stuck	stuck
strike	struck	struck
sweep	swept	swept
swim	swam	swum
swing	swung	swung
take	took	taken
teach	taught	taught
tear	tore	torn
tell	told	told
think	thought	thought
throw	threw	thrown
understand	understood	understood
wake	woke	woken
wear	wore	worn
win	won	won
write	wrote	written

WORDLIST

adj = adjective, adv = adverb, n = noun, v = verb,
pv = phrasal verb, prep = preposition, exp = expression

Note: There is space for you to write other words you would like to learn.

Unit 1

absent *adj* not in a place, especially school or work

advise *v* to tell someone they should do something

apologise *v* to say you're sorry

bring up *pv* to look after a child until he or she becomes an adult

can't stand *v* to dislike something or someone very much

canteen *n* a restaurant in an office, factory or school

drama *n* a play in a theatre or on television or radio

environmentally friendly *adj* not damaging the environment

e-pal *n* somebody you write to on the internet but haven't met

facilities *n* buildings or equipment that are provided for a particular purpose, e.g. a swimming pool, tennis courts, etc.

fond of *adj* liking something a lot

hand in *pv* to give work to your teacher

look forward to *pv* to feel happy and excited about something that is going to happen

persuade *v* to make someone agree to do something by talking to them a lot about it

recipe *n* a list of foods and a set of instructions telling you how to cook something

warn *v* to tell someone not to do something because something bad may happen

My words

....

....

....

....

....

....

....

....

....

Unit 2

achieve *v* to succeed in doing something difficult

ambition *n* a strong feeling that you want to be successful or powerful

athlete *n* someone who is good at sports such as running, jumping or throwing things

beat *v* to do something better than has been done before

believe in *pv* to feel confident that you or a person is good or right

BMX biking *n* a sport where people ride special bicycles on special tracks

champion *n* someone who has won an important sports competition

championship *n* a competition to find the best player or team in a sport

competitor *n* someone who takes part in a sports competition

defeat *v* to win against someone in a fight or competition

disappointment *n* the feeling of being disappointed

diving *n* the activity or sport of jumping into water with your arms and head going in first

fail *v* to not be successful

get in *pv* to succeed in entering a place, especially a building

give in *pv* to accept that you have been beaten and agree to stop competing or fighting

have a positive attitude *exp* to have good opinions or feelings about something

join in *pv* to become involved in an activity with other people

lose *v* If you lose a game, the team or person that you are playing against wins.

luck *n* good and bad things caused by chance and not by your own actions

polite *adj* behaving in a way that is not rude and shows that you think about other people

respect *n* when you are polite to someone, especially because they are older or more important than you

rude *adj* behaving in a way which is not polite and upsets other people

score *v* to get points in a game or test

stay in *pv* to stay in your home

succeed *v* to do something that you have been trying to do

surfing *n* the sport of riding on a wave on a special board

talent *n* a natural ability to do something

win *v* to get the most points or succeed in a competition

My words

....

....

....

....

....

....

....

....

....

....

Unit 3

a market stall *n* a table used for selling things at an outdoor event

bracelet *n* a piece of jewellery that you wear around your wrist

casual *adj* casual clothes are comfortable and not formal

changing room *n* a room in a shop where you can try clothes

delayed *adj* happening at a later time than expected or intended

employ *v* to pay someone to work for you

end up *pv* to be in a place or state because of doing something

fancy dress party *n* at a fancy dress party, the guests all put on funny clothes and dress as, e.g. characters from a film

fashionable *adj* popular at a particular time

forbidden *adj* not allowed by an official rule

iron *n* a heavy hot object that you use to make clothes smooth

material *v* cloth used for making clothes

maximum *n* the largest in amount, size or number that is allowed

request *v* to ask someone to do something in a polite or formal way

sandals *n* shoes with open toes you wear in the summer

sew *v* to join things together with a needle and thread

silk *n* a type of cloth which is light and smooth

stripes *n* a line of one colour on a background of another colour

stylish *adj* attractive and fashionable

top *n* a piece of women's clothing worn on the upper part of the body

My words

....

....

....

....

....

....

....

....

....

....

Unit 4

afraid *adj* frightened or worried

annoyed *adj* angry

anxious *adj* worried and nervous

band *n* a group of musicians who play modern music together

challenging *adj* difficult, in a way that tests your ability or determination

comedy *n* a funny film or play

concert *n* a performance of music and singing

disappointed *adj* unhappy because something didn't happen or something wasn't as you expected

drums *n* a musical instrument that you hit with your hands or a stick

enjoyable *adj* If something is enjoyable, you like doing it.

entertaining *adj* interesting and helping someone to have an enjoyable time

excited *adj* feeling very happy and interested

festival *n* a series of special events or performances

flute *n* a musical instrument that you hold out to the side and play by blowing

guitar *n* a musical instrument with strings that you play by pulling the strings

jealous *adj* not happy because someone else is better at something or has something you want

organised *adj* well prepared and carefully planned

perform *v* to act, sing, dance or play music for other people to enjoy

piano *n* a big wooden musical instrument with black and white bars that make sounds when you press them

relaxed *adj* calm and not worried

relaxing *adj* If something is relaxing, it is pleasant and makes you feel relaxed.

satisfied *adj* pleased with something you have done

scary *adj* frightening

science fiction *adj* stories about life in the future or in other parts of the universe

serious *adj* meaning what you say, not making a joke

stage *n* the raised area in a theatre where actors perform

surprised *adj* feeling surprise because something has happened that you did not expect

trumpet *n* a metal musical instrument that you play by blowing into it

venue *n* a place where a sports game, musical performance or special event happens

violin *n* a wooden musical instrument that you hold against your neck and play by moving a stick across strings

worried *adj* unhappy because you are thinking about bad things that might happen

My words

....
....
....
....
....
....
....
....
....
....

Unit 5

allowed *adj* have permission to do something

beef *n* the meat from a cow

boiled *adj* cooked in hot water

cabbage *n* a large, round, hard, green vegetable with lots of leaves that you eat raw or cooked

cod *n* a type of fish

corn *n* a long vegetable made up of lots of yellow seeds

fit *adj* healthy, especially because you exercise a lot

forbidden *adj* not allowed by an official rule

fried *adj* cooked in hot oil or fat

frozen *adj* frozen food is very cold and has been frozen so that it will last a long time

go back *pv* to return to a place where you were or where you have been before

go for *pv* to choose

go on *pv* to continue doing something

go up *pv* to become higher in level

healthy *adj* making you strong and not ill

lettuce *n* a green vegetable with lots of soft green leaves that you use in salads

peach *n* a fruit that has a soft skin and is yellow/pink and has a yellow inside with a large seed

permit *v* to allow something

pineapple *n* a tropical fruit that is large, yellow and with a thick yellow-brown skin with sharp points on it

raw *adj* not cooked

require *v* If a rule requires something, you must do that thing.

responsible *adj* in charge of someone or something

spinach *n* a green vegetable with dark green leaves that are cooked or eaten raw in salads

strawberry *n* a small soft red fruit with lots of seeds on the outside

tuna *n* a type of fish

turkey *n* a large bird like a chicken

yoghurt *n* a food made from milk that is thick and slightly sour (= not sweet)

My words

....
....
....
....
....
....
....
....
....

Unit 6

cosy *adj* comfortable and warm

cultural events *n* exhibitions, films and concerts are examples of cultural events

elderly *adj* elderly people are old

gallery *n* a public building where people can look at works of art

ladder *n* a thing which you climb up when you want to reach a high place, which has two long pieces joined together by shorter pieces

sociable *adj* someone who is sociable likes being with people and meeting new people

stone *n* a hard, natural substance that is found in the ground and often used for building

storm *n* very bad weather with a lot of rain, snow, wind, etc.

tent *n* a structure for sleeping in made of cloth fixed to metal poles

My words

....
....
....
....
....
....
....
....
....
....

Unit 7

bat *n* a small animal like a mouse with wings that flies at night

cage *n* a container made of wire or metal bars used for keeping birds or animals in

calm *adj* If the weather or the sea is calm, it is quiet and peaceful.

camel *n* a large animal that lives in hot, dry places and has one or two humps (= raised parts on its back)

carry on *pv* to continue doing something

clear *adj* If the sky is clear, there are no clouds.

climate change *n* the way the Earth's weather is changing

cruel *adj* very unkind, or causing people or animals to suffer

desert *n* a large, hot, dry area of land with very few plants

elephant *n* a very large, grey animal with big ears and a very long nose

environment *n* the natural world including the land, water, air, plants and animals

flood *n* when a lot of water covers an area that is usually dry

gorilla *n* a big, black, hairy animal, like a large monkey

humid *adj* humid air or weather is hot and slightly wet

jungle *n* an area of land in a hot country where trees and plants grow close together

keep on *pv* to continue doing something

litter *n* pieces of paper and other waste that are left in public places

mild *adj* When the weather in winter is mild, it is not cold.

mosquito *n* a small flying insect that drinks your blood, sometimes causing a disease

ocean *n* one of the five main areas of sea

oil *n* a thick liquid that comes from under the Earth's surface and that is used as a fuel

parrot *n* a bird with feathers of many bright colours that can copy what people say

pass on *pv* to give someone something that someone else has given you

penguin *n* a large, black and white sea bird that swims and cannot fly

pollution *n* damage caused to water, air, etc. by bad substances or waste

protect *v* to keep someone or something safe from something dangerous or bad

rare *adj* very unusual

recycling *n* when paper, glass, plastic, etc. is put through a process so that it can be used again

river *n* a long, natural area of water that flows across the land

shark *n* a large fish with very sharp teeth

snake *n* a long, thin creature with no legs that slides along the ground

spider *n* a creature with eight long legs which catches insects in a web (= structure like a net)

sunset *n* when the sun disappears in the evening and the sky becomes dark

tiger *n* a large wild cat that has yellow fur with black lines on it

waterfall *n* a stream of water that falls from a high place, often to a pool below

whale *n* a very large animal that looks like a large fish and lives in the sea

wildlife *n* animals, birds and plants in the place where they live

My words

....

....

....

....

....

....

....

....

....

Unit 8

astronaut *n* someone who travels into space

boarding card *n* a card that a passenger must have to be allowed to enter an aircraft or a ship

float *v* to move gently through the air

harbour *n* an area of water near the coast where ships are kept

platform *n* the area in a railway station where you get on and off the train

seasick *adj* feeling ill because of the way a boat is moving

speed limit *n* the fastest speed that a car is allowed to travel on a particular road

submarine *n* a boat that travels under water

traffic jam *n* a line of cars, trucks, etc that are moving slowly

weigh *v* to measure how heavy someone or something is

My words

....

....

....

....

....

....

....

....

....

....

Reading • Part 1

Questions 1 – 5

Look at the text in each question.
What does it say?
Mark the correct letter **A**, **B** or **C** on your answer sheet.

Example:

0

> PASSENGERS PLEASE NOTE:
>
> THERE IS A DELAY OF 10 MINUTES
>
> ON TRAINS TO EXETER

A Trains to Exeter are all ten minutes late.

B The train journey to Exeter takes ten minutes.

C The next train to Exeter will arrive in ten minutes.

Answer: 0 **A** B C

1

> Andrew,
>
> My dad's not taking me to the
> volleyball match tonight – I'm sick,
> so we can't give you a lift as promised.
> Could your dad drive you instead?
> Call me,
> Max

A Max wants to know if Andrew's dad can drive them both to the match.

B Andrew is asking whether he can have a lift to the match with Max.

C Max is suggesting Andrew's dad may have to take Andrew to the match.

2

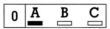

ABC CINEMA

ALL THIS WEEK – *Starstruck*
Saturday / Sunday: Student
reductions (ID card required)

A There is a special showing of *Starstruck* for students on Saturday and Sunday.

B To see *Starstruck* more cheaply, go at the weekend with your student card.

C It's possible for students to see *Starstruck* at a reduced price all this week.

3

To: Ben
From: Martin

I'm thinking about what subjects to study at college. Computer Science looks interesting, but I don't know much about it. I'd really like your opinion!

Martin is emailing Ben to

A ask for advice about a college course.

B tell Ben his decision about a subject.

C make a suggestion to Ben about studying.

4

Maria,
Mum wanted me to go shopping after school and get vegetables for tonight's supper. She forgot I'm going swimming – could you do it instead?
Let me know!
Sean

A Sean is hoping that Maria will do him a favour.

B Maria has to prepare supper after school tonight.

C Mum has asked Sean to help her instead of going swimming.

5

To: All students
From: Mrs Anderson
School concert practice: all actors taking part should attend, and also musicians – we're short of those! Art students – thanks for painting the stage!

For the concert, Mrs Anderson needs more students who

A know how to act.

B are willing to help with the stage.

C can play a musical instrument.

Questions 6 – 10

The people below all want to find some caves that they could visit.
On the opposite page there are descriptions of eight caves to visit.
Decide which caves would be the most suitable for the following people.
For questions **6–10**, mark the correct letter **(A–H)** on your answer sheet.

6

Marek and his family often visit caves, so would prefer not to have a guide. They'd like to find caves with interesting rock shapes, and where they could have a swim.

7

Jane and her family want a tour of caves that look just as they did when they were discovered, with original cave paintings. They like caves with water flowing through them.

8

Mario and his family will be visiting caves during the winter, and don't want anywhere cold inside, or very small. They'd like to have someone show them the caves and explain their history.

9

Twins Henry and Karina are keen on photography and want to take good pictures inside and outside the caves they visit. Their parents would like to attend a music performance inside the caves.

10

Justine and her family are experienced at visiting caves, and want to find some that go a long way underground. They'd also like to see an exhibition about how the caves were discovered.

Caves to visit

A   Hatton Hole
The area here isn't attractive, but the temperature inside is comfortable – there's even a stream for swimming! These caves have been made larger for the music shows held here. Cave paintings can be seen further underground, and there are books available about the caves' history.

B   Mara Hollow
You'll need to know all about going into caves to visit this place, as there's no guide. You can walk comfortably for hundreds of metres, but some sections are quite narrow. There's a great display of the caves' history, with paintings and photos showing the first people to enter the caves during the 20th century.

C   Maribu Caves
These caves are perfect for experienced people wishing to visit caves by themselves, as they're quite safe. And there's plenty to see as the colourful rocks inside look like strange objects – animals, birds or even vegetables! There's also a big natural pool you can dive into, so take your costumes!

D   Trussack Cavern
These huge old caves go underground for miles, and when the temperature drops outside, it's actually warmer inside! The guides know everything about the caves, from how they were used thousands of years ago, to their recent discovery. The natural swimming pool and scenery outside are beautiful – perfect for photos.

E   Kemble Caves
You'll need a guide round these caves. They're not deep, but they're narrow, with streams running through them. However, the rock shapes you'll see hanging from the roof are amazing! The views outside are beautiful, and there's a great exhibition about people living in the caves centuries ago.

F   Dragon's Nook
These caves are surrounded by beautiful trees and waterfalls. They were made larger recently to let visitors enter easily, and they're now big enough to hold exhibitions and concerts – from pop to classical! Visitors can walk around without a guide. Take your camera for the original wall paintings!

G   Sorian Hill
This is a great place for a swim! Waterfalls flow into rocky pools outside the entrance. Inside, rock has been removed to make a wonderful space for visitors, although photography isn't allowed in here. Classical music plays as you walk around by yourselves.

H   Cabran's Den
These large, deep caves with waterfalls are perfect for photos of the strange rock shapes. There are pictures on the rock walls done by people living here centuries ago, who'd find the caves nowadays haven't changed at all – including the low temperatures! Visitors are accompanied by guides.

Questions 11 – 20

Look at the sentences below about a dog called Rusty and his travels.
Read the text on the opposite page to decide if each sentence is correct or incorrect.
If it is correct, mark **A** on your answer sheet.
If it is not correct, mark **B** on your answer sheet.

11   The text says dogs are better than other animals at finding their way to unfamiliar places.

12   Rusty the dog seems to understand that he has to wait patiently to get on trains.

13   When he arrives in the city centre, Rusty has a routine that he follows every day.

14   Rusty is often so hungry that he will eat any kind of biscuits he is offered.

15   After visiting the corner shop, Rusty goes back home because he is full.

16   At first, Rusty had problems getting on the train with no ticket.

17   Station staff have been concerned for some time that Rusty might get lost on their trains.

18   Rusty became famous after he suddenly seemed to disappear for a few days.

19   One TV viewer insisted he knew where Rusty had been while he was away.

20   The corner shop has become very popular due to Rusty's visits.

Rusty's Travels

Throughout history there have been lots of stories about animals and how clever or brave they can be. Take, for example, all the films about dogs, cats and other animals making amazing journeys to find their owners after they've become lost. But dogs are also known to be particularly skilled at persuading people to feel sorry for them and give them food when they're hungry!

One dog has shown himself to be especially good at both finding his way around and getting food. Every morning Rusty the dog goes down to his local railway station. He gets in a queue with all the other passengers to board the train from the suburbs where he lives, and then rides into the city centre. When he gets there, Rusty jumps off the train and goes off to the shops. He always goes around all his favourite food shops, where he's given special things to eat. First stop is a corner shop, where he has hand-made biscuits that the owner gives him every morning for his breakfast. 'He's quite particular,' says the owner. 'He'll only accept his favourite biscuits and refuses any others I try to give him. Even though I'm sure he's hungry, he's just not interested!'

Then later in the morning, Rusty goes over to his friend the restaurant owner, where he gets a plate of food for his lunch. When he's eaten everything, Rusty makes his way home on the train.

When Rusty first started making this trip, station staff refused to allow him to get on the train without anyone to accompany him or buy a ticket for him. But then they felt sorry for him and have now given him a free ticket, because they've been so impressed by his cleverness at finding his way around the city's complicated transport system without getting lost.

However, at one stage Rusty worried all his friends in the city by failing to appear at his favourite eating places for several days. This started a search for the missing dog, and his picture was shown in newspapers and on TV. Rusty finally returned to find he'd become a TV star. 'He's obviously been off on an adventure,' said one TV viewer, 'but Rusty's not telling anyone what he's been up to!'

The corner shop owner was certainly glad that Rusty was back. 'Thanks to the publicity I've got through Rusty, my shop's full of customers – and they all want to buy some of Rusty's favourite biscuits!'

Questions 21 – 25

Read the text and questions below.
For each question, mark the correct letter **A**, **B**, **C** or **D** on your answer sheet.

Being a triplet
by Desiree Matloob

As soon as people realise that my brother Michael, my sister Tiffany and I were born on the same day, that we're triplets, they ask the strangest questions. But no, we can't read each other's minds. We don't have the same dreams. And I can promise you that we don't always get along. These are the things I get asked most often when people meet me for the first time.

Although there are lots of good things about being a triplet, one thing I really don't like is when people think of us as one person – 'MichaelDesireeTiffany' instead of 'Michael' and 'Desiree' and 'Tiffany'. I don't like it when people think we should act or think the same just because we were born at the same time, like when people ask me why I'm so shy while Michael and Tiffany are so much louder. And I definitely don't like it when people don't understand that we have individual likes and dislikes.

Growing up, Tiffany, Michael and I shared almost everything. It was funny how the exact moment I wanted to use the bike was the same time that Tiffany felt like going for a ride. When the three of us learned to drive at the same time, we constantly fought over who got to practise with the car.

My dad came up with a brilliant plan called 'turns'. One Saturday a month, each of us would have a chance to spend three hours with our dad, alone, and do whatever we wanted. For three hours every month each of us was allowed to feel like he/she was an only child. This helped me to see that being a triplet is a part of me, but it isn't the only part of me. I don't just want to be thought of as 'Desiree, the girl who's a triplet'. I want to be thought of as an individual.

21 Why is Desiree writing this article?

    A to give her personal opinion about being a triplet

    B to explain what makes being a triplet exciting

    C to describe some of the problems all triplets face

    D to show the good and bad side of being a triplet

22 When people ask her about being a triplet, Desiree feels surprised that they

    A have never met a triplet before.

    B always want to know the same things.

    C don't already know the answers.

    D are so interested in triplets.

23 One thing that annoys Desiree about being a triplet is when people

    A confuse her with her brother and sister.

    B think her brother and sister should be similar to her.

    C always want to meet her brother and sister.

    D are unable to remember their individual names.

24 What does Desiree say about 'turns'?

    A It was the only time she had any individual choice.

    B She thought three hours a month was not long enough.

    C She enjoyed having all her dad's attention.

    D She realised how lucky only children are.

25 Which of the following advice for parents of triplets would Desiree agree with?

A
> Encourage triplets to have different hobbies and to spend time away from each other. They need to have space to develop their own interests.

B
> You need to help triplets to see themselves as individuals. They don't often just look the same, they think in the same way too.

C
> The good thing is that you won't need to buy separate toys; triplets often find it easy to share things from a young age.

D
> Don't expect your triplets to get on well. Triplets often fight a lot because they feel jealous of each other but this passes as they grow up.

Questions 26 – 35

Read the text below and choose the correct word for each space.
For each question, mark the correct letter **A**, **B**, **C** or **D** on your answer sheet.

Example:

0	**A** by	**B** of	**C** on	**D** in

Answer:

0	A	B	C	D
	▬	▭	▭	▭

How bees communicate

Bees have a special kind of language; they communicate **(0)** .... dancing. The worker bees that **(26)** .... honey communicate in this way more than most other kinds of bees. Every morning, worker bees **(27)** .... off to find food. When they find some, they return home to **(28)** .... the other bees know where it is. They do this by **(29)** .... different dances.

If the worker bees find food **(30)** ...., they do one type of dance. **(31)** .... if the food is further away, they do a different dance. The type of dance also shows which way the bees **(32)** .... fly to find the food. And the length of the dance shows **(33)** .... far it is. A short dance shows there isn't far to go. The speed of the dance also **(34)** .... important information; dancing **(35)** .... fast means there is a lot of food.

26	**A**	develop	**B**	produce	**C**	create	**D**	invent
27	**A**	start	**B**	set	**C**	put	**D**	get
28	**A**	inform	**B**	explain	**C**	let	**D**	allow
29	**A**	appearing	**B**	playing	**C**	acting	**D**	performing
30	**A**	nearby	**B**	next	**C**	around	**D**	approximately
31	**A**	As	**B**	So	**C**	But	**D**	Since
32	**A**	need	**B**	have	**C**	ought	**D**	should
33	**A**	just	**B**	how	**C**	yet	**D**	only
34	**A**	gives	**B**	tells	**C**	brings	**D**	takes
35	**A**	totally	**B**	completely	**C**	extremely	**D**	absolutely

Questions 1 – 5

Here are some sentences about a party.
For each question, complete the second sentence so that it means the same as the first.
Use no more than three words.
Write only the missing words on your answer sheet.
You may use this page for any rough work.

Example:

0   Anna's birthday is July 25th.

     Anna was .... July 25th.

Answer: | **0** | born on |

---

1   Anna invited all her friends to a party at her house.

     All .... invited to a party at her house.

2   Anna invited more friends to this year's party.

     Anna didn't .... friends to last year's party.

3   There was so much food they couldn't eat it all.

     There was too much food .... to eat.

4   Most of Anna's friends went home at 10.30 p.m.

     Most of Anna's friends didn't .... 10.30 p.m.

5   Anna's mum asked if she had enjoyed the party.

     Anna's mum asked, '...................... the party, Anna?'

Question 6

You have just won an essay writing competition. Write an email to your English-speaking friend, Sam. In your email, you should:
- explain how you found out about the competition
- tell Sam what your essay was about
- say what you received as a prize.

Write **35 – 45 words** on your answer sheet.

Write an answer to **one** of the questions (**7** or **8**) in this part.
Write your answer in about **100 words** on your answer sheet.
Mark the question number in the box at the top of your answer sheet.

Question 7

- This is part of a letter you receive from your English friend, Denise.

> Our art teacher has just given us a project to do –
> the topic is 'The City'. But I don't know what to draw
> or take photos of – have you got any ideas? Write and
> tell me!

- Now write a letter to Denise, giving her some ideas for her project.
- Write your **letter** on your answer sheet.

Question 8

- Your teacher has asked you to write a story.
- Your story must have the following title:

    An unexpected visitor

- Write your **story** on your answer sheet.

Questions 1 – 7

🔘 40 There are seven questions in this part.

For each question, choose the correct answer **A**, **B** or **C**.

Example: What do the students agree needs replacing in their school?

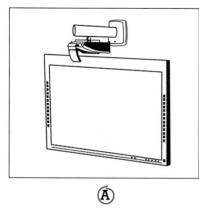  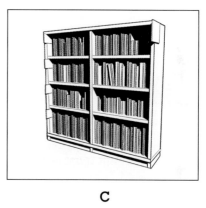

Ⓐ   B   C

1   What must the boy do after school?

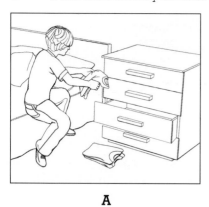  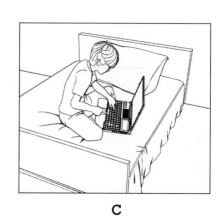

A   **B**   **C**

2   What time did the girl's new swimming lesson finish?

 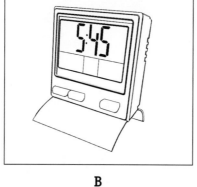 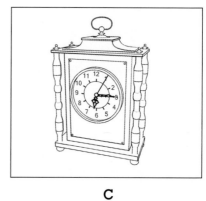

A   **B**   **C**

3 Which animal was the film about?

A

B

C

4 What is the boy going to buy at the market?

A

B

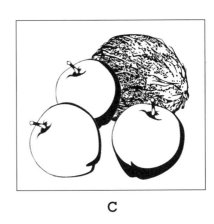

C

5 What will the weather be like on Saturday?

A

B

C

6   What happened to the boy at the basketball match?

A

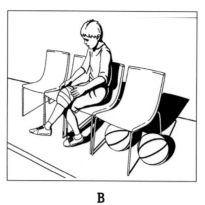

B

C

7   What does the girl still want to buy for the party?

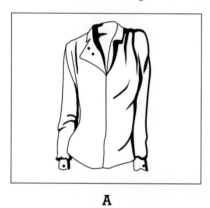

A

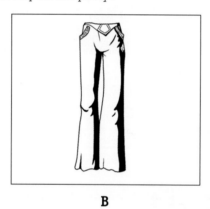

B

C

Questions 8 – 13

🔊 41 You will hear an interview with an Australian girl called Verity, who has recently been on a student exchange programme. For each question, choose the correct answer **A**, **B** or **C**.

8 Verity chose the Netherlands for her exchange programme because

  A a friend had recommended it.

  B one of her relatives was from there.

  C she had always wanted to go there.

9 What did Verity find difficult about living in the Netherlands at first?

  A sharing a bedroom

  B getting up early

  C cycling to school

10 What did Verity immediately notice about the Netherlands?

  A The countryside was more varied than Australia.

  B The buildings were how she'd imagined them.

  C The weather was much colder than she'd expected.

11 What was different about the school in the Netherlands?

  A It had better facilities.

  B There was a wider range of subjects.

  C The class size was much bigger.

12 Verity was surprised that students in the Netherlands

  A knew very little about Australia.

  B had never considered doing an exchange programme.

  C had travelled to a lot of countries.

13 Verity recommends that students on an exchange programme should

  A go to a place where they can speak the language.

  B stay for six months.

  C ask their parents to visit.

Questions 14 – 19

🔊 42 You will hear a boy called Jake talking to his classmates about a diving trip he recently did with his family.

For each question, fill in the missing information in the numbered space.

DIVING TRIP

Jake's only previous diving experience was in a **(14)** ....

Jake went for his first sea dive off the coast of **(15)** ....

Jake's **(16)** .... went into the water with him.

Jake says the best thing he saw under the water was a **(17)** ....

Jake enjoyed swimming with some **(18)** .... in the sea.

Jake managed to do **(19)** .... dives in total.

Questions 20 – 25

🔊 43 Look at the six sentences for this part.
You will hear a conversation between a boy, Harry, and a girl, Laura, about wildlife photography.
Decide if each sentence is correct or incorrect.
If it is correct, put a tick (✔) in the box under **A** for **YES**. If it is not correct, put a tick (✔) in the box under **B** for **NO**.

		YES	NO
20	Harry admires the wildlife photo of a fish in *Animals* magazine.	A	B
21	Harry thinks the unusual creatures in Laura's photos are what makes them good.	A	B
22	Laura and Harry find it's hard to keep still when taking wildlife photos.	A	B
23	Harry doubts whether his camera is good enough for wildlife photography.	A	B
24	Laura thinks it's important to get up early to take wildlife photos.	A	B
25	Laura and Harry are both considering getting more instruction in photography.	A	B

(2–3 minutes)

Phase 1
Good morning / afternoon / evening. I'm ...
What's your name?
What's your surname?
How do you spell it?
Where do you live?
Do you study English at school?
Do you like it?

Phase 2
(possible examiner questions)
What did you do yesterday evening?
Tell us about what you enjoy doing with your friends.
Which sports do you enjoy playing or watching?
Tell us about the food you enjoy eating.

Speaking • Part 2

(2-3 minutes)

Interlocutor
I'm going to describe a situation to you.

A boy and his sister are **going on a camping trip** in the **mountains** next week. Talk together about the **things they will need** on the camping trip, and decide which are the **most important** things to take.

Here is a picture with some ideas to help you.

(3 minutes)

Interlocutor

Now I'd like each of you to talk on your own about something. I'm going to give each of you a photograph of people **relaxing**.

Candidate A, here is your photograph. Please show it to Candidate B, but I'd like you to talk about it. Candidate B, you just listen. I'll give you your photograph in a moment.

Candidate A, please tell us what you can see in your photograph.

Now, Candidate B, here is your photograph. It also shows people **relaxing**. Please show it to Candidate A and tell us what you can see in the photograph.

(3 minutes)

Your photographs showed people **relaxing**. Now, I'd like you to talk together about the different ways you relax alone and with other people.

Candidate C

Acknowledgements

Author acknowledgements
The authors would like to thank their editors Judith Greet, Clare Nielsen-Marsh and Ann-Marie Murphy for their useful input and hard work. Many thanks also to Linda Matthews (production controller), Michelle Simpson (permission controller), Hilary Fletcher (picture researcher), Leon Chambers (audio producer), Darren Longley (proof reader).

Sue Elliott would like to give thanks to her lovely children for their tolerance, and to her co-author Amanda for her help and support.

Publisher acknowledgements
The authors and publishers are grateful to the following for reviewing the material during the writing process:
Susan Wilkinson: France; Cressida Hicks, Jane Hoatson, Jessica Smith, Catherine Toomey: Italy; Laura Clyde, Sarah Hellawell: Spain; Cagri Gungormus Yersel: Turkey; Katherine Bilsborough, Annie Broadhead, Felicity O'Dell, Rebecca Raynes, James Terrett: UK.

Development of this publication has made use of the Cambridge English Corpus (CEC). The CEC is a computer database of contemporary spoken and written English, which currently stands at over one billion words. It includes British English, American English and other varieties of English. It also includes the Cambridge Learner Corpus, developed in collaboration with the University of Cambridge ESOL Examinations. Cambridge University Press has built up the CEC to provide evidence about language use that helps to produce better language teaching materials.

This product is informed by the English Vocabulary Profile, built as part of English Profile, a collaborative programme designed to enhance the learning, teaching and assessment of English worldwide. Its main funding partners are Cambridge University Press and Cambridge ESOL and its aim is to create a 'profile' for English linked to the Common European Framework of Reference for Languages (CEFR). English Profile outcomes, such as the English Vocabulary Profile, will provide detailed information about the language that learners can be expected to demonstrate at each CEFR level, offering a clear benchmark for learners' proficiency. For more information, please visit www.englishprofile.org

Text acknowledgements
The authors and publishers acknowledge the following sources of copyright material and are grateful for the permissions granted. While every effort has been made, it has not always been possible to identify the sources of all the material used, or to trace all copyright holders. If any omissions are brought to our notice, we will be happy to include the appropriate acknowledgements on reprinting.

Text on p. 107 adapted from 'Stray Dog commuter wins free rail pass', source: Annanova, from http://www.newsforthesoul.com/01dec/12-01dog-train.htm; LA Youth for the text on p. 108 adapted from 'Would you believe we're triplets' by Desiree Matloob, http://www.layouth.com/would-you-believe-were-triplets/. Copyright 1998-2012 L.A. Youth. L.A. Youth is a publication of Youth News Service (YNS). Reprinted with permission.

Photo acknowledgements
The authors and publishers acknowledge the following sources of copyright material and are grateful for the permissions granted. While every effort has been made, it has not always been possible to identify the sources of all the material used, or to trace all copyright holders. If any omissions are brought to our notice, we will be happy to include the appropriate acknowledgements on reprinting.

T = Top, C = Centre, B = Below, L = Left, R = Right, B/G = background

Grammar header: iStockphoto/ManuelBurgos; Listening header: iStockphoto/coloroftime; Reading header: iStockphoto/artpipi; Speaking header: iStockphoto/drbimages; Writing header: iStockphoto/DNY59; Vocabulary header: Cambridge University Press/Cambridge Advanced Learner's Dictionary, 2005.

p. 6: Thinkstock/Getty Images/Jupiterimages/Goodstock; p. 7 (1): Thinkstock/Medioimages/Photodisc; p. 7 (2): Thinkstock/Photodisc/Kevin Peterson; p. 7 (3): Thinkstock/Getty Images/Jupiterimages/Photos.com; p. 7 (4): Thinkstock/iStockphoto; p. 7 (5): Thinkstock/Photodisc/Amos Morgan; p. 9: CUP/Trevor Clifford; p. 10: Thinkstock/Fuse; p. 12: Shutterstock/Aleksandr Bryliaev; p. 14 (BCR): Lehtikuva OY/Rex Features; p. 14 (BR): Actionplus/Daniel Swee; p. 14 (CL): Thinkstock/iStockphoto; p. 14 (BL): Rex Features; p. 14 (BCL): Rex Features; p. 14 (C): Getty Images/Jeff Siner/Charlotte Observer/MCT; p. 14 (CR): Getty Images/Cameron Spencer; p. 15: Getty Images/Hannah Johnston; p. 17: Getty Images/Ezra Shaw; p. 19: Alamy/©James Nesterwitz; p. 23 (CL): Alamy/©Janine Wiedel Photolibrary; p. 23 (C): Corbis Super RF/Alamy; p. 23 (CR): Alamy/©economic images; p. 23 (B): Alamy/©Alex Segre; p. 24 (CL): Thinkstock/Photodisc/Amos Morgan; p. 24 (BL): Rex Features/Ray Tang; p. 24 (BR): Alamy/©David Anthony; p. 25: SuperStock/©Loop Images; p. 28 (CL): Shutterstock/Luna Vandoorne; p. 28 (CR): Thinkstock/Purestock; p. 28 (B): Thinkstock/Brand X Pictures; p. 29: Alamy/©Design Pics Inc; p. 30 (TR): Getty Images/Stone+/Adrian Weinbrecht; p. 30 (B): SuperStock/©Cultura Limited; p. 31: iStockphoto/izusek; p. 35: Rex Features/Startraks Photo; p. 36 (C): SuperStock/©Marka; p. 36 (R): Shutterstock/Vitalliy; p. 37: Alamy/©vario images GmbH & Co.KG; p. 38 (CL): Thinkstock/iStockphoto; p. 38 (C): Getty Images/The Image Bank/Alan Thornton; p. 38 (CR): ArcticPhoto/©B&C Alexander; p. 44: Shutterstock/Goodluz; p. 45: Corbis/©Heide Benser; p. 46 (BL): Alamy/©David South; p. 46 (C): Alamy/©Peter Alvey; p. 46 (BR): Thinkstock/Getty Images/Jupiterimages/Photos.com; p. 47: Alamy/©Kumar Sriskandan; p. 48: Getty Images/The Image Bank/Yellow Dog Productions; p. 49 (R): Alamy/©Jeff Morgan 01; p. 49 (TC): Alamy/©2ebill; p. 49 (BC): Alamy/©Alex Segre; p. 50 (1): Shutterstock.com/Rob Wilson; p. 50 (2): Shutterstock.com/Rudolf Tepfenhart; p. 50 (3): Thinkstock/iStockphoto; p. 50 (4): Shutterstock.com/Hogar; p. 50 (5): SuperStock/©Steve Vidler; p. 55: Alamy/©Jim Corwin; p. 56: Shutterstock.com/Rat007; p. 58 (1): Alamy/©Robert Fried; p. 58 (2): Thinkstock/Comstock Images; p. 58 (3): iStockphoto/kate_sept2004; p. 58 (4): Thinkstock/Digital Vision/Ryan McVay; p. 58 (5): Getty Images/Image Source; p. 60 (BL): Shutterstock.com/Sura Nualpradid; p. 60 (BR): Alamy/©Photoshot Holdings Ltd; p. 61: Getty Images/AFP/Sam Yeh; p. 62 (L): Thinkstock/Purestock; p. 62 (CL): Alamy/©Shaun Finch-Coyote-Photography.co.uk; p. 62 (BR): Shutterstock.com/topseller; p. 62 (R): SuperStock/©imagebroker.net; p. 62 (Sarah): Photoshot/©Monkey Business; p. 62 (James): iStockphoto/BunnyHollywood; p. 62 (Mark): Thinkstock/Getty Images/Jupiterimages/Creatas; p. 63: SuperStock/©Robert Harding Picture Library; p. 65: Getty Images/Bloomberg/David Paul Morris; p. 66 (BL): Thinkstock/Creatas Images; p. 66 (BCL): Shutterstock.com/Natali Glado; p. 66 (BC): SuperStock/©Steve Vidler; p. 66 (BCR): SuperStock/©Photononstop; p. 66 (BR): Alamy/©van hilversum; p. 67 (BL): SuperStock/©Eye Ubiquitous; p. 67 (BR): Rex Features/LEHTIKUVA OY; p. 68: Getty Images/AFP/Mark Ralston; p. 104 (6): Thinkstock/Ron Chapple Studios; p. 104 (7): iStockphoto/JBryson; p. 104 (8): Thinkstock/Getty Images/Jupiterimages/Comstock; p. 104 (9): GettyImages/Eric Audras; p. 104 (10): ImageSource/Blend Images; p. 107: Rex Features; p. 122: SuperStock/©Blend Images; p. 123: Getty Images/Taxi/Karen Moskowitz; p. 127: Getty Images/Iconica/Andersen Ross.

Illustrations by:
Maxwell Dorsley (New Division) pp.6, 18, 32, 39, 56, 81; Richard Jones (Beehive Illustration) pp. 12, 51, 66, 78; Kate Rochester (Pickled Ink) pp. 13, 21, 22, 40, 53, 64, 85, 91, 121; Laszlo Veres (Beehive Illustration) pp.34, 52, 54, 76, 87, 89, 114, 115, 116;

Design, layout and art edited by: Wild Apple Design Ltd.